Praise for *Let It Be Easy*

"When your brain is an uninspired, chaotic place to live, reach for *L*⸺ ⸺ *v*. Susie Moore's genuine kindness, compassion, and excitem⸺⸺ ⸺ ⸺ ⸺ humans reach their utmost potential beam throu⸺ and heart-wrenching personal stories. Each ⸺ we're all getting A's."

— Ashley Oe⸺

"The title says it all! *Let It Be Easy* is not only inc⸺ ⸺⸺y to read, it's full of eye-opening, no-BS, to-the-point wisdom to ⸺ ⸺⸺ all areas of your life. This book is a must if you're looking to reduce friction in your life and find joy!"

— **Kate Northrup**, bestselling author of *Do Less*

"Susie Moore's lighthearted storytelling style makes it easy to absorb deep lessons and makes it simple to remember them as needed. You'll return again and again to the messages she offers, such as making good decisions and finding affluence, and you'll discover that hope is always possible."

— **Farnoosh Torabi**, editor-at-large of CNET and host of the podcast *So Money*

"Susie Moore is open, honest, and vulnerable — challenging readers to embrace ease instead of stress despite the craziness of the world we live in. It leaves stressed-out overachievers with a special message: Everything doesn't have to be so hard. You can have success and ease in the same breath."

— **Kimberly B. Cummings**, author of *Next Move, Best Move*

"If you keep thinking, 'Life shouldn't be this hard,' Susie Moore's *Let It Be Easy* is the book for you. These nuggets of wisdom will help you relax and find a simpler way through virtually any dilemma you face."

— **Michael Hyatt**, *New York Times* and *Wall Street Journal* bestselling coauthor of *Win at Work & Succeed at Life*

"My friend Susie Moore always gives the best advice, and *Let It Be Easy* is no exception. Susie's latest book will give you the tools to reclaim your happiness and confidence regardless of what life throws your way — yes, even a pandemic."

— **Candace Nelson**, pastry chef and judge of *Cupcake Wars*

"Susie Moore's lighthearted, story-driven approach to navigating the complexities of life has a lot to offer the modern reader. Her practical, to-the-point lessons are approachable, memorable, and a great reminder to 'let it be easy'!"

— **Sanni McCandless**, life coach and cofounder of OutWild

"Susie Moore's *Let It Be Easy* philosophy is life-changing. I love the way she moves through the world with ease and elegance. Every modern woman needs to read this book!"

— **Anna Bey**, elegance expert and YouTube personality

"Part shaman, part therapist, 100 percent inspiration. Susie Moore has used her jaw-dropping life story to provide a moving, practical, sensational guide to letting everything be easier. Shockingly easier. Like you can't believe it could be so easy. Like the first sigh of relief you've breathed in years! Let go of doing things the hard way! Stop pushing boulders uphill! *Let It Be Easy* is packed with gems that will transform everything about how you move through the world. If you have been 'a struggler,' look no further than your heaven-sent Master Teacher of Ease and her handbook for life on the easy road."

— **Sheri Salata**, former executive producer of *The Oprah Winfrey Show*

"Any compilation of insights into universal topics that can actually surprise readers with new ideas is an instant treasure. This one's for all of us."

— **Mike Dooley**, *New York Times* bestselling author of *Infinite Possibilities*

"*Let It Be Easy* is a book for anyone who has felt alone, anxious, or tense. It's a book for those struggling with friendships or work or romantic relationships. It's a book for avid readers of self-help and for casual browsers in the bookstore; a book for the brave and for the timid; a book for reading on beaches and trains and in minutes between meetings. That is to say: it's a book for everyone."

— **Libby Kane**, executive editor of *Insider*

"Susie Moore's *Let It Be Easy* wisdom might change your life. It's changed mine. Susie's the real deal. Rush to read this book!"

— **Amy Purdy**, athlete and *New York Times* bestselling author of
On My Own Two Feet

"With every chapter, Susie Moore tackles life's challenges to help us understand how we can 'let it be easy.' In reading, you'll begin to discover all the areas in your life where you can apply Susie's extraordinary advice because she makes it that easy! I loved this book! So many chapters where I was saying out loud, 'Yes!' and, 'Gosh, she's so right!' I highlighted a million things. A must-read."

— **Amanda Kloots**, fitness instructor, cohost of *The Talk*,
and *New York Times* bestselling author of *Live Your Life*

LET IT
BE
Easy

Also by Susie Moore

Stop Checking Your Likes

LET IT BE *Easy*

Simple Ways to
Stop Stressing & Start Living

SUSIE MOORE

Foreword by RUTH SOUKUP

New World Library
Novato, California

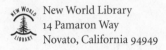

New World Library
14 Pamaron Way
Novato, California 94949

Text design by Tona Pearce Myers

Library of Congress Cataloging-in-Publication Data

Names: Moore, Susie, author.
Title: Let it be easy : simple ways to stop stressing & start living / Susie Moore ; foreword by Ruth Soukup.
Description: Novato, California : New World Library, [2021] | Summary: "Presents real-life stories that illustrate the paradoxical truth that success comes when we struggle less, stop fighting ourselves, and stay open to the opportunities that life sends our way"-- Provided by publisher.
Identifiers: LCCN 2021033361 (print) | LCCN 2021033362 (ebook) | ISBN 9781608687572 (paperback) | ISBN 9781608687589 (ebook)
Subjects: LCSH: Stress (Psychology) | Stress management. | Self-actualization (Psychology) | Simplicity.
Classification: LCC BF575.S75 M66 2021 (print) | LCC BF575.S75 (ebook) | DDC 155.9--dc23
LC record available at https://lccn.loc.gov/2021033361
LC ebook record available at https://lccn.loc.gov/2021033362

First printing, November 2021
ISBN 978-1-60868-757-2
Ebook ISBN 978-1-60868-758-9
Printed in Canada on 100% postconsumer-waste recycled paper

New World Library is proud to be a Gold Certified Environmentally Responsible Publisher. Publisher certification awarded by Green Press Initiative.

10   9   8   7   6   5   4   3   2   1

For Heath

Contents

Foreword

*A*t the start of 2020, having just emerged from one of the most difficult years of my business career, I declared that my word for the year was to be *easy*. It was an idea that came directly from my dear and brilliant friend Susie, who was constantly reminding me to "let it be easy."

She squealed when I told her I had decided to embrace this mantra, and she immediately sent me a gift to celebrate — a big red button from Staples that when pushed says "that was easy" (just like in the commercials!).

It has sat on my desk ever since, a daily reminder of a mantra that has become such a powerful force in my life that I now wonder how I ever lived without it.

Let it be easy.

Because at the start of 2020, who could have even begun to predict the level of chaos, stress, and disruption that we would face in a year unlike any other in our recent history? Who could have known we'd be locked down for months, isolated from friends and family, unable to travel, and needing to wear masks in public? Who could have known that our entire way of life would be altered so abruptly and completely?

Say what you will about 2020, but the one thing it was not was *easy*.

And yet, that one simple phrase — *let it be easy* — changed everything for me. But to understand just how much, I have to back up a little, to mid-2019, when my business very nearly imploded, and I along with it.

The ironic thing is that from the outside, no one would have known how much I was struggling. It looked like I was at the top of my game, embracing the jet-set life of a successful influencer. I had just published my sixth bestselling book, *Do It Scared*, along with a groundbreaking new Fear Assessment that was the culmination of more than two years of research. I spent more time on planes and in hotels than at home, always for the sake of more publicity, more elbow rubbing, and more opportunities. I even managed to snag an invite to Necker Island, where I sat right next to Richard Branson at dinner.

From the outside, my life looked like a dream come true.

But I was living a nightmare. Because the reality was anything but glamorous. Behind the scenes, I was working harder than ever, waking up early, staying up late, ignoring my family and friends, struggling to manage this beast of a company I had created. I had grown it so fast, in so many different directions, that it seemed impossible to tame. On top of that, I had allowed the people I had hired to make one bad decision after another while I worried about more publicity.

I was stressed to the max, and downright angry — angry at the people I had trusted who had let me down, but mostly angry at myself for letting it happen.

Susie was one of the few voices of reason in the midst of my self-created storm. Again and again, she encouraged me to stop fighting so hard, to stop overcomplicating my life and my business, and to start allowing things to just flow. And so I did.

It wasn't easy at first. When complexity is what you're used to, a lifetime of making things harder than they need to be is a challenging habit to break. But I kept coming back to the mantra. *Let it be easy.*

I cut my team in half, from eighteen down to nine. I simplified my business and began focusing on the few activities that would have the biggest impact rather than trying to do it all. I began making decisions based on profit, not ego. I stopped traveling, stopped exhausting myself, and stopped worrying about what other people might think. I started having fun again, started allowing myself to really be present in my life, and began enjoying more time with my family and friends than ever before.

I let it be easy.

And now I find myself looking back with nothing but gratitude for Susie and this simple but powerful force she casually dropped into my life, perhaps without even knowing it. Because despite all the hardships the year has brought, both my business and my family life are stronger and healthier than ever. Not only that, but I'm the happiest and most content I've ever been. Compared to where I was eighteen months ago, it feels like a miracle.

As you read this amazing book, I encourage you to open

yourself up to the power of ease and begin embracing this mantra in your own life.

Dare to let it be easy.

Because make no mistake — it's going to take courage.

It takes courage to cut through the noise and eliminate the unnecessary.

It takes courage to choose simplicity over complexity.

It takes courage to stop fighting and to start trusting.

It's worth it.

— **Ruth Soukup,** *New York Times* bestselling author of
Living Well, Spending Less

Introduction

I've lived through some terrible things in my life,
some of which actually happened.

— MARK TWAIN

*I*f your life could be made easier, what would that be worth to
you?

When my husband, Heath, almost left me, I went to a therapist. Our arguments had swelled to the point where he was finished with my ever-shifting shrieking criticisms of him.

This is the right way to spend a weekend.

That's the wrong way to spend money.

I can't believe you told that couple personal business of ours.

Heath's withdrawn energy made my body ache with sadness.
Our marriage was so close to being over, I had already begun
planning in my mind my move back to the UK, imagining how

I'd ask my boss for a transfer to the London office. My world felt unsteady and horrible.

I needed help. Therapy was my last resort. After one especially bad fight — followed by a night Heath spent sleeping on the sofa — I went to the first shrink I could find on Google. I splashed hot water on my face so my cheeks would look flushed, told my boss I had a fever, and walked to the therapist's office, praying I could be fixed somehow.

Heath wasn't the only person who was sick of my need for control over everything — frankly, I felt exhausted, too. I was just twenty-seven, and we were only a year into our marriage, but I was so weary of myself. I had no idea I had formed an allegiance to my own suffering, and part of me was unknowingly addicted to the stress I was creating in my life.

I didn't understand it. I'd read loads of self-help books. After consuming self-help material pretty much every single day since I was fifteen, I knew the principles of managing your mind: Gratitude first. Take responsibility for your life. Think big. Focus on what you want. Forgive everyone. Take nothing personally. Love yourself.

When I arrived at the therapist's office, I was too exhausted to censor my words. I told the truth — about Heath's night sleeping on the sofa, the fighting, my despair. All of it.

Google had done me well — my new therapist was warm and good-humored. His kind eyes peered over the rims of his cheerful green spectacles as I told him about my inability to relax and my Olympian-level skill of feeling on edge (and therefore starting fights) over small things. Nodding his head, he said to me, "That must be hard on you — having to control so much. And on top of that, you have to be Heath's keeper! No wonder you're in my office."

"Well, yes! As his wife, his suffering is very important to me," I joked.

I *was* being too hard on Heath, which drove me to this pleasantly air-conditioned office. But what about me? The way I'd been behaving sucked for me, too. The enemy was inside the gates! What if the problem wasn't things "going wrong" on the outside but, in fact, *me*?

I looked happy. I took pride in wearing chic blazers in meetings, I enjoyed dinners out with pals, and I was always smiling in the Friday-night downtown Manhattan dinner pics that were posted online. But when I was alone, I felt a low-level anxiety that wouldn't budge.

Do you ever feel that way? Anxious or on edge about something — work, money, relationships, your health, other people's opinions? That it's never just ... *easy*? And as a result, your natural response is to react, worry, control, and seek perfection?

"In every marriage — even a days-old marriage — you can seek out grounds for divorce," Dr. Green Eyeglasses said. "The trick is to find and continue to find grounds to stay married. That doesn't come when we're hard on each other. It comes when we give our partner — and *ourselves* — grace. Especially during difficult times. Could there be another way for you to be in your marriage?"

His gentle words opened what felt like an iron gate within me. *Another way?* It reminded me of *A Course in Miracles*, which states, "There is another way of looking at the world," followed by, "I could see peace instead of this."

It was by no accident that right about that time I also came across a quote from one of my favorite authors, Wayne Dyer, who said, "There is no stress in this world, only stressful thoughts." And I heard speaker and author Esther Hicks say, "When you believe something is hard, the universe demonstrates the difficulty. When you believe something is easy, the universe demonstrates the ease."

Huh.

I'm creating stress so successfully all by myself? It was a revelation to me. The idea of "another way" was both shocking and freeing. Because I knew that if I am the problem, I am also the solution.

It was like all the self-help I'd consumed and struggles I'd overcome could only take me so far without this critical piece of wisdom. The real prize of the experience and education I'd given myself over the years still required one further step: be aware that we (unconsciously) create most of the stress in our lives. I can drop the sword! I can relax! I can see the world and myself in a more gentle and compassionate way. When stress bubbles up (and it does!), I began to question how necessary the stress was instead of just believing it was required. This very act alone is life altering. I ask, is this problem real or imagined? Do I need to control or resist the circumstances before me right now? Can this problem go away just by seeing it through a let-it-be-easy lens?

Enter ease.

Ease needs a good lawyer; it's not represented very well out there. Which is exactly why this book exists — to break down the *let it be easy* philosophy and give you direct, practical, real-life ideas on how to let ease in.

I mean, who questions hardship? People say being married

is hard, being single is hard, making money is hard, not making money is hard, being a parent is hard, not having kids is hard, working is hard, not working is harder... you get the idea. Anything especially good or valuable must be hard, hard, hard. How can a human enjoy their limited time on planet Earth when it's "so hard" out there?

Think for a moment: Do you expect hardship and stress in your life? I've discovered that this line of thinking is the sneakiest, most invisible, and most common form of self-sabotage there is. Because it's a lie that few people question. When it sunk in that I could consciously disinvite the "life is hard" lie, I started to look at my life in a new way. It was like nothing and everything changed at once. Because I changed. Peace and ease had to begin with me. Slowly I began to become comfortable controlling less in the external world. I went inside myself more. It soothed me on the inside. Counterintuitively, the external world improved. A lot.

If I felt the need to start an argument or point out a flaw, I began to pause for a second instead of just reacting. And before diving into a stressful situation, I'd think, "Aha. This is a moment when I'd normally step in and push or force something. What's an easier way?" Often, it was simply doing nothing. Ease shows up like a small miracle each time we remember that it's available to us.

Please don't worry if you are skeptical that your life can be easier. You're not alone. It can take some time to turn dogma around. Growing up, were you among the many kids who genuinely believed in Santa? If you were, think back to when you found out Santa was a beautiful creation and not a reality. Did you need years of counseling to reprogram your mind to the truth? *Ho, ho, ho, no!*

Maybe the transition to more ease can be just as instantaneous. Because when you pay attention, you'll notice that a lot of the best things in your life actually *found you*. Ease already exists in your life, even if you overlook it.

Maybe fertility wasn't a challenge for you. Perhaps you easily landed the funniest, most loyal friends years ago. Maybe elegant outfits just come together in your closet or you can whip up a decent meal from limited ingredients. Big or small, whatever comes easily to you, you might unknowingly be taking it for granted.

But you're still *letting it be easy* without knowing it. Because you don't fight it.

As a life coach, I hear different problems from different kinds of people all the time. But despite the range of specific issues and circumstances, the underlying issue is often the same: an unexamined belief that we have to earn our worth and that every good thing is somehow meant to be hard.

Let it be easy wisdom runs counter to this. And it applies to everything — what to make for dinner, how to have more intimacy with your spouse, how to manage a crisis, the best way to make peace with a neglectful parent. *Everything!* You can always allow more ease in. It's like a puppy outside the glass door. It wants *in*.

Letting it be easy is not about toxic positivity or an unhealthy denial of real pain. Also, to be clear, it's not about denying that terrible things happen all the time and that human beings face huge challenges. Prejudice of all kinds exists, particularly racism, ableism, sexism, ageism, classism, homophobia: the list is real and goes on and on. But what I *am* saying is that a lot of the time we make life harder on ourselves by sabotaging those areas that we *do* have control over.

"Pain is inevitable, but suffering is optional," as the old saying goes. Part of *letting it be easy* is realizing you can't control what happens to you, but you can control how you respond. You can choose how you direct your energy and not make hard situations harder.

The core purpose of your life is to enjoy it. Even when I was six years old, living in various shelters and on welfare, I knew this. At that age, I had not yet discovered how hard the world I lived in *should* be, given my circumstances. If only we could be as easy as we were as children! The *let it be easy* philosophy is therefore more of an *unlearning* than a new learning.

This book will help you allow more good things into your life. You'll naturally attract more of what you want to be, do, and have. When you let it be easy, your life won't be flawless, but it will be considerably better. And when people see the shift within you, everyone's going to want to know your secret.

Heath and I celebrated eleven years of marriage this year. Our relationship isn't perfect, but he sometimes tells me he's had two wives: "Before Susie" and "Now Susie." I sometimes wonder where "Before Susie" would be if she hadn't learned what I share with you here.

Flip through this book as it calls to you. You don't need to read the chapters in any particular order. Nothing but your willingness to see your life in an easier, gentler way is needed. You're reading more than just words on a page. You're reminding yourself of the truth of who you really are.

Let it be easy.

Yours in love,

Susie

Xx

Nature Is Proof
That Ease Surrounds Us

"*W*hat grows together, goes together."

Oh, I thought. *That's a sweet little line.* And what made it even more special was the fact that I was a bit in awe of the person who said it to me.

A chef who used to work at Per Se, Thomas Keller's famous three-Michelin-star restaurant in New York, was giving us a cooking lesson. We'd never been to Per Se because the price tag scared us — the tasting menu costs more than $300 a person — but here my husband, Heath, and I were, hanging out with a top chef. We were spending the weekend at a luxury resort called Blackberry Farm in Tennessee, a trip we'd won as a prize.

Naturally, I expected this famous chef's cooking to be difficult and sophisticated, packed with exotic ingredients and finicky steps that were hard to execute. *Should I bring a notepad?* I'd wondered.

Turns out, I didn't need to.

"People overcomplicate what makes a good meal," the chef

told us. "The best thing you can do is to use fresh, in-season ingredients, and then just keep it simple with olive oil, lemon juice, a pinch of salt."

He smiled as he whipped up a tomato, basil, and cucumber salad, which he piled high on a delicate bone-china plate.

"Make your salads tall, friends," he chirped. "No depressing flat salads allowed!"

It's true, right? Restaurants serve things vertically — tall salads, tartares, ice cream sundaes. It adds to the fancy.

Could that be it? Could cooking be that simple, especially given that you pay more than $20 for a salad like this in a fancy place? Is it *enough* to just use what you're given — combined with the passion and inclination to create that comes from within?

Apparently so, because you're given the right ingredients at the right time. All you have to do is roll up your sleeves and trust that fresh ingredients from the garden out back grow — *and therefore go* — together.

The chef went on to say that any onion can be used in a recipe to replace a particular type of onion listed as an ingredient. And honey and maple syrup can often be used in place of sugar. Nature is overflowing with ways to make our lives a little easier, it seems. The chef was joyful in the way he spoke as he sliced and sprinkled, using his hip to close the drawers, passing the basil around so we could all get a whiff of the summery scent. Fancy stuff can even be free-flowing and flexible.

Wow. I'd made cooking so hard by building it up to be complex. I'd grown up believing that you must sweat in the kitchen to get a good result (I mean, you gotta *earn* it, right?). And therefore

I ended up not doing much in the kitchen at all — besides keeping my Pellegrino chilled and a bowl of pretzels topped off.

Is there an area of your life where you're doing this? Overcomplicating something that *wants* to be easy? Waiting? Missing out before you've even begun?

As the chef spoke about five-star cuisine, it was like he was revealing some ancient truth about the universe at large: keep it simple. Nature's creations and timing are perfect. Don't make it hard when it can be fun. Let life be easy and good.

If ease and excellence coincide in the kitchen, where else can that be true? It turns out — everywhere.

2

Add to Your Plate

*M*y friend Tracy, a health and fitness coach, always loads up her plate with a rainbow of colorful vegetables — mesclun salad greens, sweet bell peppers, crunchy carrots, thinly sliced beets — before putting anything else on it.

"Crowd out the less-good-for-you stuff!" she laughs.

It makes sense, right? *Fill yourself up with what's good for you.*

I applied this rule in a new context when I noticed that a few of my friends were feeling like less-than-positive influences in my life. For a while, I'd focus on them, how and why I felt unsupported by them, and worried about why they couldn't share my joy when good things happened for me.

It was confusing and frustrating. I spent more time alone as a result — and in a resentful way. My plate was full of food that didn't taste right anymore and that ultimately wasn't all that healthy.

After a period of dissatisfaction, I decided to add new people to my life. I went to new events, joined different communities, and opened myself to new groups. I didn't have to empty my plate or complain about what was on it; what was there naturally just got "crowded out" by new additions. This made me happy, and it seemed so obvious all of a sudden.

When you expand what's on your plate and what brings you joy, no one thing is the source of your happiness. And no one person or thing can take away your joy. We've all known someone who is utterly wrapped up in their work, and if they lose their job, they feel like their life is over. It's the same with someone wrapped up in a relationship. When their partner leaves, it feels like there's nothing left.

The truth is, if someone feels that way, *their plate was full of just one or two ingredients. It didn't have enough variety. They were eating one color, not a rainbow.*

We live in an inclusive universe. Add more. Say yes to more. Be open. Be curious. Be easier about new, different, and better options for you. Instead of obsessing over what's missing from your plate or what you don't like, *add to your plate.* You don't have to stick to the same old choice just because it's familiar. Experiment with new food and flavors. Observe all the options. Life's a menu. Switch it up!

3

Volume Creates Victory

*W*hy is JLo, JLo? Dolly Parton, Dolly Parton? Daymond John, Daymond John?

It's not because they've released one album each or invested in one company each. They've released *tons* of albums and launched *loads of companies.*

They create a lot. Fail a lot. Remember the JLo movies *Gigli* and *Jersey Girl*? Probably not! They were widely considered to be some of the worst films ever made. What about Dolly's movie *Rhinestone*? The film was panned on its release and was regarded as a commercial and critical flop. In his book *The Power of Broke*, Daymond John tells of throwing a massive party on a boat, scraping together $20,000 to create an event with the hope that it would put him on the map. But the event was a flop, and he ended up losing everything.

We just don't hear about the failures because that's not what we see and not what most people want to talk about — failures more often than not remain behind the scenes. People who are truly successful don't dwell on them (or at least, not for long). They keep moving forward.

Observe any super successful person. They have a huge bias toward action, and there are no exceptions. They get busy. They say yes to more. They simply do and create more. Their faith is supported by (a lot of) action.

JLo has eleven albums and has been in forty-five movies.

Dolly has fifty-seven albums. Fifty-seven! More than a hundred, if you count compilation albums.

John has invested in sixty-plus businesses (and this is just on-the-air investments).

It's not about trying once and then stopping.

It's constant forward motion.

How much you create is not for others to decide. You get to decide!

When I meet someone who says, "Oh yeah, I tried that, and it didn't work," I know why. They stopped way too soon. Maybe the average person tries something two to three times before giving up and claiming they're not meant for it. Success and failure are on the same road — success is just further down that road.

When you get the win that you've been holding out for, the countless times you tried before that won't mean a thing. One success will compensate for all the perceived failures.

Success is driven by volume — it's not destiny reserved for a special few at birth. It's not about sweating it out to create the one perfect thing. Dialing up the volume is possible for absolutely everyone. Isn't that a relief?

4

The Best and Fastest Way
to Change Someone

"*O*kay," I said. This simple, two-syllable utterance improved my marriage in an instant. In one final moment of ease and nonresistance, I dropped a battle I'd been fighting for a decade.

My husband looked shocked. Then he said, "Cool! I'll be in my office for a bit, okay?"

Soon I heard loud gunshots and victory whoops emanating from behind his office door as he played with a pack of other online gamers.

Heath likes to play video games from time to time. For years, I'd teased him about it and would fight with him about what I perceived as a pathetic, uncool habit. Video games just felt juvenile to me. I wasn't being judgmental *at all* (smiley face)! For a long time there, I thought that these games were just unacceptable for a grown man.

But then I had to level with myself. I was on my high horse about video games, and why? Was I reading books on chess strategy and watching Ingmar Bergman films in my spare time? (Not that that would be an excuse for snobbery!) Nope — I read self-help books and watch *The Real Housewives of Beverly Hills, New York, Atlanta,* and *Orange County.* And *The Bachelor* and *The Bachelorette.* And *Bachelor in Paradise.* I think we can all agree that *The Bachelor Winter Games* was boring. And these are hobbies that are *cough* far ... more acceptable, wouldn't you say?

For context, my first husband was a gambling addict and gambled away what little money we had. Now *that* was something I couldn't shrug off — nor should I have. Anyone related to an addict knows the roller-coaster ride you feel you're on and how serious it can become. And the truth is, Heath is the opposite of an addict.

He wasn't at a casino. Or even at a bar with his friends not responding to my texts. He was in the other room, decompressing after a stressful day.

I had to recognize that I don't have any of the "three-A" issues in my marriage (addiction, abuse, and adultery). And given that my marriage is overall a healthy one, I decided to question myself about my knee-jerk loathing of video games. Heath is a good husband, so why exactly can't he kill digital baddies — or whatever the heck gamers do online — for two hours on a Saturday afternoon?

Maybe you're annoyed that your partner:

- refuses to meditate — and you know the magic of meditation!
- spends too much time consuming the news or talking about politics.
- eats too much junk food.
- runs late all the time.

Trying to change someone else is a major cause of strain in relationships. Many people believe something along the lines of "I need my partner to behave a certain way for me to feel good, and when I don't feel good, it's their fault."

But here's another approach: "Do you. I'll be over here, feeling good and loving you no matter what."

Which attitude would you prefer being directed at you?

Think about it for a moment: What's something you would like to change in yourself? An unhealthy habit? Gossiping? Overeating or overdrinking? Procrastinating? Always being late or failing to follow through on the goals you set?

Changing yourself is hard, right? *Then why on earth would we think it's a good idea to try to change anyone else?*

When I said okay to Heath's gaming, besides being shocked, he was so surprised, he fell absolutely silent. And less than a couple of hours later, he walked out of the office, stretching his back, with a look on his face that was cute and loving. And ultimately, we want our partners to feel loved, right?

It's not up to me to sanction what Heath does with his time. By giving him a simple okay, I helped build intimacy in our home. We could've spent months in therapy for me to accept it, but this was much easier (and saved money and time, to boot).

Only one person needs to *let it be easy* for a relationship to improve. Can it be you?

5

You Are Bigger Than
What's Making You Anxious

*W*hen I was in high school, there was a cool girl a few years older than me who didn't like me. Her name was Rosa.

She once shrieked "Fake!" at me in the hallway when we passed each other between classes. She and her Marlboro Light–smoking posse gave me dirty looks whenever I saw them. And I pretended not to notice. A friend of mine whose sister was in said posse told me that Rosa said I was "so dumb and annoying."

As a thirteen-year-old, I was upset and confused. What did I do wrong? I had never even spoken to Rosa — how could I annoy her? And how could I make this reason to dread school go away?

I avoided her to minimize annoying her.

Anyone who has dealt with high school drama knows how consuming it can be. I thought about Rosa on every train ride and long walk to school, and thinking about what she might say next gave me stomachaches, especially on Sunday nights.

Rosa was the center of my worries. Rosa ruled my teenage world.

And then ... we moved. As soon as I started at my new school, Rosa was a distant memory. Within half a day in a new uniform, in a new classroom, in a new town, life was all about my new friends and new crushes and what was cool in *this* school. I've never forgotten the golden lesson of perspective that swift change gave me.

Your immediate community (school, college, industry, place of work, mom group, town, church, book club, IG following) is only one of *many* communities that exist. But we forget that. We're so consumed being in whatever communities we already know, that if something goes wrong, we think, "That's it! I'm done for!" The world seemingly collapses. When every community — no matter how big — is only ever one of millions.

I once knew a woman (an acquaintance of my mother's) who tried to commit suicide when her husband left her for another woman. Not only had the wife lost her marriage, but her friend circle dropped her as they remained friends with her husband and started becoming friendly with "that bitch replacement." The wife's community abandoned her. That's a difficult and awful thing to cope with, and I can only imagine how alone and betrayed she felt. Your community can feel like your entire world, and when it's pulled from you, you can feel disoriented and desperate. It's like the death of an old life, and that takes time to grieve. And for her, that was nearly it.

Contrast this story with that of a woman I coached a few years back. She was of a similar age when her husband left her. But instead of giving in to despair, she took her small divorce settlement and moved to California, something her ex-husband would never do. She then remarried within two years. Her Instagram feed is awash in happy photos of herself and her husband running through Palisades Park in Santa Monica. I always get a kick out of seeing her thrive.

I once worked with a guy who was fired because of drunken behavior at a corporate conference. This could be a career ender, right? Well, he swiftly left the advertising industry and simply moved into another field instead. Last I saw on LinkedIn, he's doing just fine. It's as simple as that! New community, new life.

Our communities feel all-engrossing, and they can be incredibly valuable. They can give structure and meaning to our uncertain world, and it's nice to feel like we belong to and feel safe in them. But if you step back for a second, you'll realize that lots of communities exist in the world. And you can have a place in many.

The truth is, your current life is just one version out of many, many potential versions. Anytime you want, there are opportunities to start over. While it may be difficult and scary at first, you can give yourself a new place, new friends, a new career, a new climate, whatever you want. Whenever you review your many life options in any situation, you feel at your most powerful. There are options everywhere, all the time. The choice is yours.

It's a great reminder not to despair.

You and your potential are more significant than what feels insurmountable. Just know that what feels enormous and heavy to you is nothing compared to the endless possibilities that lie before you. You're way more free than you realize.

6

Living Your Dreams
Can Start Right This Second

*F*inding, living, and fulfilling your life's purpose can feel like *heavy* work. We have all these dreams inside, but they can feel big and unreachable and confusing. I mean, how the heck do we get from *here* to *there*? A magical day will come, right, when we achieve our dreams? Or a fairy godmother will descend from a pink cloud out of the sky? Maybe we'll have a perfect moment of clarity on a retreat in the Himalayans — you know, when you can make a retreat work with the kids' schedules, your demanding job, and your partner who hates being left alone, and when you've saved tons of money and your to-do list clears up.

Good news for you: living your dreams is simpler than that. Your life is happening right now. *As you read these words. This moment is your life.*

Write out five big dreams you have for your life.

For example:

1. Truly see the world, in an unrushed way. Visit my dream destinations, most important, Italy, Egypt, and Vietnam.

2. Have a deep, intimate, and physically satisfying relationship with my partner.
3. Write a book.
4. Be in the best shape I can be in. Invest in looking fantastic and feeling healthy.
5. Have real, close relationships with friends I laugh and enjoy life with.

Now, write out what your past five days looked like — and be honest!

1. Just tried to make it through the week! Shuttling kids around, feeling rushed and irritated. Haven't even thought about (much less planned and saved for) a dream vacation.
2. Nagged my partner for being late and leaving socks around the house. Forgot to kiss him goodbye yesterday.
3. Watched twenty-three hours of TV.
4. Drove everywhere. Ate pizza and went to bed without washing my face.
5. Scrolled Facebook. Didn't call anyone I care about. Kept meaning to plan a happy hour with friends but collapsed on the sofa with my phone every night instead. Scrolled Facebook, again.

Is your day-to-day supporting what you actually want? Life isn't about "getting through the week." Life is in session! This ain't no dress rehearsal.

This simple exercise can be a loving shake into realizing we're out of sync with what we want and value the most. If your top five dreams are the most important things to you, can you spend a little time each day on them? There will never be a better time. *It's never about right timing, it's about conviction. And you owe it to yourself to have more conviction.*

With ease, can you:

- put a little money aside each month into your "Europe next year!" vacation account?
- plan one nonnegotiable date night a week? (A babysitter and dinner out are cheaper than therapy and divorce, let me tell ya.)
- write thirty minutes a day by getting up half an hour earlier?
- work out? Just do it! And don't skimp on skin-care products! Get the best you can afford. You're worth it (and not because L'Oréal said so).
- plan one night out with your friend group a month? You can start a text chain right this second.

None of it has to be perfect; it just has to be in motion. Simply do your best, and ask yourself, *Can I realize my dreams in an easy, small way today?* I know you can. Why wait?

Living your dreams can be simpler than you think. Don't underestimate the magic of small things.

7

If Something Feels Off,
It Probably Is

g dated a guy once who was just not that into me. Instead of saying so, he kept the sex coming with statements like, "Why be 'boyfriend and girlfriend' — why not just be us? Much more real."

It was confusing and ... just felt off. But I worried I was being demanding and uptight.

Another time, a new friend asked me if I wanted to invest in a real estate opportunity with him. I asked how it worked. He dazzled me with fancy expressions like "ROI" and "compounding" and "market growth" and hey — I was into it — for a minute. But a queasiness accompanied my interest (oh, that clever intuition!). You know that feeling — like, you just woke up from a bad dream you don't remember but the heaviness of it still lingers?

I tried to explain to Heath what *exactly* was being offered to us, and I couldn't. I felt silly, as it screamed scam. Not shockingly, I didn't speak to my new "friend" again after I turned the deal down.

Life is not supposed to be complicated. Avoid gray areas. If something feels off — it probably is. Relationships, investments, everything in life should be easy to explain … even to a kid. If you can't, maybe you're approaching a sharky zone. Swim away!

8

It's Okay to Be Sad after Making the Right Decision

I separated from my first husband when I was just twenty-two. Although our divorce was months in the making (he was a gambler, I was a control freak — you can imagine the fights), the time leading up to my leaving was incredibly sad. One morning, after I knew the end was nigh but hadn't yet told anyone — perhaps even before I had faced the truth myself — I remember waking up at around 7:00 a.m. The first thing I did was count how many hours I'd need to be awake before I could go back to sleep again. I counted fourteen to fifteen hours and then just... cried.

I was desperate and lost and sad. In my lowest moments, I didn't want to be awake or conscious at all. I bought a lot of cheap chardonnay and started drinking as early in the day as felt reasonable (some days noon, or, well, 11:45 a.m. because we're being honest with each other here).

A friend of mine who divorced her husband after his countless infidelities says that even though they coparent in a good-enough way, she feels so sad sometimes going into her daughter's room when she's with her dad. As she tidies up, just seeing her daughter's Barbies, projects, and posters and knowing that her daughter will be spending 50 percent of her childhood without her mom … is sad.

And that's okay. She still made the right decision for her own survival and peace. And subsequently, for her daughter's.

We can handle sadness. We can feel the emotions fully. Sadness is part of the human experience. What's easy and what's right are not always the same thing. Sadness doesn't make something wrong. It makes us human. It shows we love. And that is a beautiful thing.

9

What to Remember
When You Mess Up

I was walking my dog in downtown Miami one evening, when
I noticed a lovely restaurant and bar gleaming by the water-
front. Fairy lights, a palm tree–rimmed courtyard, soft jazz playing, servers in crisp white shirts — it was enticing.

I saw a couple of small dogs inside and, registering that it was
a dog-friendly place, shimmied up to the bar and took an empty
seat, placing my little Yorkshire terrier, Coco, on my lap.

"An Aperol Spritz, please!" I ordered enthusiastically.

The bartender smiled as he smoothly placed down my drink.

And then he asked me for my member card.

Member card?!

It was a private membership club for people with boats. I had
never heard of this place. And I am boatless.

"Uh, I'm new to the neighborhood," I said, wide-eyed. "I just
walked in from the street. I thought this was —"

"It's okay," he answered kindly, "you didn't know."

I smiled and relaxed instantly at those three gentle words.

You didn't know.

How reassuring. How easy and forgiving and kind.

It made me wonder — because I have thought of this kind encounter many times since — could we say these words more to ourselves when we make a mistake? Or when somebody else does?

Sometimes we just don't flippin' know! Can we show ourselves a little more self-compassion and grace? It's not your job to know everything. You're not Google.

I used to be so hard on myself for starting my business "late." I wished I had a head start on the entrepreneurship game like the many twenty-somethings I met once my business was in full swing.

But guess what? I didn't know. At the time, I thought getting a good job was the thing. But then I learned more. And as Maya Angelou says, "When you know better, you do better."

Before you've had the chance to learn something — which can take years, lots of challenges, and all sorts of circumstances to reveal itself — can you forgive yourself for not knowing?

And then once you know better — act!

Life is not all about knowing everything and being perfect. That would be impossible. Life is about the learning process — which can be very sweet, if you let it be. There have been many instances when I've implemented a new strategy in my business that has increased revenue to a whole new level or made a process more efficient. When this happens, I could be frustrated with myself and say, "Argh! Susie, if only you'd done this sooner! You've missed out on so much money and/or spare time as a result!" Sure, I could beat myself up about it. Instead, however, I try to show myself some grace by saying, "I didn't know before, but I'm thrilled I do now!"

Pedro the lovely bartender let me finish my drink — and he gave it to me on the house. (I left him a nice tip — as much for the life lesson as for the cocktail!)

Not knowing is normal and fine. There's no sin committed from learning. Next time you make an innocent mistake, say it with me: "I didn't know."

And then ... you do.

10

Call Your To-Do List
Your "Get-to-Do" List

*E*very day, I scrawl "Get to Do" in my journal. I *get to* run to
FedEx to return my lovely Rent the Runway dresses. I *get to*
cook lamb for my husband (two wins — having a cute husband
who enjoys my cooking and, well, *roast lamb*). I *get to* run a coaching call because I have beautiful, paying clients who have placed
their trust in me. I *get to* go to the ob-gyn because I have access
to health care, which I don't take for granted when so many other
people don't. I *get to* write this book you're holding.

See how it feels different? Nothing on your list changes. You're
just tapping the always-available-to-you appreciation filter.

11

Ordinary Routines Create Extraordinary Results

"*I*t's just so hard to remain enthusiastic all the time," a friend texted me once. She was frustrated with her business growth and was trying hard to raise another round of funding — meaning she's in constant sales mode. I had to laugh when I read her message, as I was just about to head into yet another podcast interview to promote my last book. My work is my biggest passion — but it doesn't mean that I don't get tired sometimes, too. I'd been on the circuit for eight weeks at that point, I felt like I was on my four hundredth interview of the day, and I was more than a little tired of hearing myself talk.

People come to me for motivation, thinking that I'm 100 percent enthusiastic and inspired 24-7. But I'm not.

"Have a break and get back to it tomorrow. I'll call ya then," I texted back.

Because here's what I know:

1. Humans need breaks. We're worthy of taking them without explanation or apology.

2. If you want to stay enthusiastically on track, you must remember that all the mundane, repetitive things you do each day *are leading somewhere*.

It's so easy to forget these two facts — especially the second one. When we see just the daily to-do list ahead of us, it's hard to remember the bigger picture. It's like we're looking at the asphalt road and the white lines, not the view ahead. Pause and ask yourself: *Why did I start a business/a family/a project/a fill-in-the-blank?*

Because deep inside, you hold a beautiful vision for it. The same way I hold a beautiful vision for my books — and this requires me to talk about them a lot. And how does a vision come to be, exactly? Action by action, day by day, bit by bit. A vision coming to life is driven by your daily, consistent actions that make it real. *Because anything you want to do well, you must do often.*

Life is largely routine. Can you remember where it's all leading? Remember your vision in the mundane present. I know that's easier said than done! Review your goals for just thirty seconds every morning, if that's all you can squeeze in.

No matter how tiresome your day-to-day is, can you see beyond the routine? Can you remember that it's all leading somewhere? Can you remember to look up at the windshield, not down at the asphalt?

Even when you're tired, even when it feels like too much, even when it feels pointless or when you're having a bad week/month/year.

Because when you remember that it's all leading somewhere, your day-to-day tasks don't feel so uninteresting. Sometimes just getting up in the morning and carrying on is brave. And when it feels like your vision is a long way off, remember how far you've already come. I'll bet you any money that you are further along than you give yourself credit for.

Ordinary routines create extraordinary results. Ask anyone who's successful at anything.

12

Wear Out,
Don't Rust Out, Baby

*W*hat do you think the point of your life is, really?
That's something philosophers have debated for years, but
I can guarantee you one thing — it's not to make it through to
the end without a scratch! "Look, Ma! I made it all the way to the
grave in one piece, perfectly intact and safe!" Ha!

Novelist Paulo Coelho said, "The ship is safest when it's in
port, but that's not what ships were built for."

You are "safest" in bed — but you were not born for tea and
muffins and bedsores from lying down all day. You're here to create! To contribute! To be the unique *you* that did not come off an
assembly line. The you that is temporary and whole.

Are you wearing out at sea or rusting out somewhere safe?

I want to end up in the grave out of breath, with smudged
makeup, loving others and the entire world to exhaustion, a million adventures seized all within my few precious earthly years.
"Oh, Ma! What a ride! I'm tired now — goodnight!"

Much better.

13

Communicate without Confusion

*N*ot long after moving to New York City in my twenties, I met my pal Rebecca for drinks. *Ah, yes*, I thought as I walked there. *Some wine awaits. Some oysters. And ooh — this place has the best fries! Crispy, salty, perfect fries!*

Bec and I met at the bar, and we were having a great time catching up. A few sips into her second Moscow mule, I was taken aback when she asked, "Shall we get the check soon?"

Not a single french fry had passed my lips. I was so disappointed! Wasn't she having fun? Why was the evening over so soon? Was there a hurry? *I washed my hair and took the subway for this!*

She explained to me she had a dinner date so "had to jet." With a peck on the cheek she said, "Next time let's have dinner, Sus!"

And that was that. I remained there for a minute, fryless and feeling rejected (a sad combination; I hope it never happens to you). I slowly buttoned up my coat and followed her out the door. I was miffed.

I'd just moved to NYC from Sydney, where "drinks" is an un-rushed, food-included, slow affair (a bit more like it is in Miami)! "Drinks" is not just one hour. It's not *coffee*. But a few months later, after I got the hang of New York, I *was* Rebecca. I'd batch coffees and drink dates and dinner with different people in one afternoon/evening. (I love doing this — it's efficient and fun!)

One thing I'm just careful to do is set expectations in advance, however. I'll text something along the lines of, "Excited to see you tomorrow! I can stick around till 7:00 p.m. Can't wait! Xoxo."

Bec wasn't wrong that night ten years ago. Nor was I. We just had differing expectations that we didn't communicate. Often this happens when we don't think — or make the extra effort — to be specific.

- Like when Heath asks me to "fill up the Brita" and I do (but *just* enough). After seeing him shake his head more than once when getting a second glass of water, I now know it has to be filled to the brim (on the verge of spill-ing over) for me to have "filled up the Brita."
- Or when you speak to an interior designer and say "blue" but you *mean* navy, royal, or cornflower. It's an (azure-tinged) ocean of difference!
- Or when you're mad at your partner for sleeping in on your birthday because they "should know" how to behave on your special day.
- Or when booking that beach house with friends of friends, and it turns out you're daydreaming about sunrise beach runs while they still have tunes crankin' and party guests arriving at midnight.

- Or when a friend asks if she can add "a little" hot sauce to the pizza — and you end up with a blisteringly hot pie. Eep!

Any time you neglect to share expectations with a friend, a partner, a child, or a team member, issues occur through a lack of clarity. George Bernard Shaw said, "The single biggest problem with communication is the illusion that it has taken place."

It's why all-important agreements are in writing.

When you're faced with a problem, it's worthwhile to start with yourself and ask, Was I clear? And then ask questions if the other person's expectations seem mismatched.

Asking questions takes courage! But it's important because when we don't ask questions, we make wild assumptions. We can feel rejected (like I did before I tuned in to the faster-paced, New York swing of things). We can feel confused. Or hurt. We can experience a whole host of negative emotions, and we can upset others by accident.

Being clear is worth the extra effort. Because people matter. It shows respect, too.

14

You Don't Have to
Defend Yourself, Ever

*H*ave you seen the Oscar-winning movie *8 Mile*? It's about a rapper, played by Eminem, trying to break into the rap scene in Detroit. To prove himself, he has to perform in rap battles live onstage with a series of rivals who are all trying to make each other look uncool. Whoever manages to be the last person standing (to wild applause!) wins.

But the movie opens with him choking on stage, getting booed off — and he's humiliated.

I saw the film in the theater, and by the final scene, I can tell you that the audience was rooting hard for Eminem to gather up his courage and win. We want to support this character because he lowers all his defenses. His bravado dissolves as he raps about the worst parts of his life so that his rival can't use them against him. When he stops being defensive and starts being emotionally raw, that's when he finds his power.

"I am a bum ... I do live in a trailer with my mom!"

He puts the truth out there — what a way to take the wind

outta a hater's sails! — and uses self-deprecation to disarm his opponents. This is a critically underused tool — because it's where your energy is saved.

That's why I talk so openly about my lack of *any* formal qualifications. Here's my thinking: What if there's nothing to defend? *What if it's all okay?* Now, that is a soothing idea, huh? We all want to cover up *something* sometimes. But what freedom (and success) might we have if we just ... didn't?

Being defensive isn't rational. It's ego driven and emotional. It warps the situation, makes us feel like we have to protect our position and be angry at our critics. To quote *A Course in Miracles*, "In my defenselessness, my safety lies."

People who understand, understand. You can be yourself, without defense.

15

Success Is Very Unsexy

*H*eath and I were dining at a well-known New York establishment, Sushi Nakazawa — named after its founder, the famous Daisuke Nakazawa. He is considered one of the best sushi chefs in the world and trained under Jiro Ono (known from the film *Jiro Dreams of Sushi*) for more than eleven years.

His road to success started with mastering the boring basics, then repeating them. Over and over and over again. He started by learning to make the tamagoyaki (egg sushi) — and failing hundreds of times before getting it right. This is not hyperbole. He had to make this hundreds of times for it to meet Jiro's standards.

While we were tucking into the butteriest sushi on earth, I saw Chef Nakazawa monitoring the plates as they left the kitchen. He sent one back because the sushi wasn't perfectly, evenly spaced.

But remember: the years of work isn't what people post on Instagram. They post the perfect dish that's served (the one that took *years* to get right). Restaurants display their awards, not the contents of their trash cans. We see the final products and the glory, not the thankless behind-the-scenes sweat.

Sometimes we think success comes from a shiny object, a perfect connection, a stroke of luck. In fact, it's actually more boring (and as a result even simpler!) than that.

It's being consistent.

Yep.

That takes the pressure off, doesn't it? You don't have to chase, land on, or show up somewhere in order to get what you want. Because it's not just about the right place or time or about doing the right thing. It's about continuing to show up *even when nothing is working*. Or when it feels hard. Or when you don't feel like it.

Success is boring. It's doing the same things over and over again. Look at any pro — a CEO, athlete, a stay-at-home parent. A big reason they're successful? They do the same things over and over, day after day. Repetition is the key. It's not glamorous, *but the end results are*.

If you can tolerate repetition and routine and remain consistent with a positive attitude, you're a pro. Just because it doesn't feel exciting doesn't mean that you're doing it wrong or that something is missing.

What boring fundamentals are you applying to your life today? The results are sexy.

16

Drifting Off Your
Life's Course Happens Slowly

I'm not a strong swimmer. Heath likes to joke that our five-pound Yorkshire terrier, Coco, is a stronger swimmer than I. So when I get into the water at the beach, I like having a few people around me — and at least a couple further out than me, too (so if there's a shark, it'll get them first).

But one time when Heath and I went to the beach, it was so hot, I jumped straight in, while he decided to sunbathe for a bit first. The water was welcoming and warm, and I floated around for a bit, thanking God for such a wonderful morning. Then I got to some daydreaming, the usual tapping out that occurs when you're all blissed-out and relaxed.

I lost track of time, but when some seaweed grazed my elbow, I stood up, surprised. The people who had been chatting around me before were now far away. I looked at the shore and saw I had drifted in front of a totally different set of umbrellas. This made me panic a little. *I have no phone! These all look the same! Where's my husband — left or right, damn it?*

It was so easy to just ... drift away.

It can be like that in life, too, right? You can kinda *check out* for a bit. You drift along in the current, then when you stand up and look around, you might be far from where you started out, but you're not in the place you want to be.

When I noticed how far I'd drifted, thanks to those invisible currents, the shock woke me up — and helped me focus on finding my way back.

The funny thing about life is that more often than not, it's a very undramatic course of events (like soothing, quiet waves) that can take you off course. Over the years, you might not even notice that you're just letting the current pull you in a direction not of your choosing. But one day, you might think, *How the heck did I get here?*

Maybe...

You're still in a relationship that's wrong for you.

Your health and fitness are diminishing.

Your career still hasn't taken off.

That credit card debt is growing.

You and your partner have slowly stopped communicating.

Your friendships aren't satisfying.

In whatever way you've been floating along, know this: *ignorance and inertia are the enemies in your life.*

Our tendency to do nothing and look away is just as bad as consciously creating damage to ourselves and harming our lives. Here's the trick to stop drifting and start swimming to shore: *pay more attention.* Have goals, and measure yourself against them. Notice where you're going. Invisible pulls are everywhere, like currents in the ocean. But they can never rival something as simple and powerful as a clear, focused intention.

17

"Best Thing I Never Had"
Is the Best Beyoncé Song

*A*s much as I love iconic tracks like "Formation" and "Crazy in Love," in my humble opinion, it's the less-well-known song "Best Thing I Never Had" that's Beyoncé's best.

The lyrics are about avoiding a major mistake — in this song's case, getting out of a relationship with an unfaithful man before tying the knot. I especially love the lines "Thank God you blew it / I thank God I dodged a bullet / I'm so over you, so baby, good lookin' out."

Can you relate to this? Maybe not to this exact scenario, but think about it for a second. Did you ever really want something that didn't work out? And in the end, not getting what you'd dreamed of turned out to be the biggest blessing?

What if the thing you think you *should* want — marriage, a promotion, home ownership — isn't what will truly make you happy? And say you decide *not* to have it, despite what other people think is best for you. Could that, in fact, be the best thing?

I've seen a few variations of this over the years. Here are a couple of examples that might spark some recognition in you.

Planting Roots versus Having Adventures

A year or so ago, my friend Priya was heartbroken when her purchase of a flat in London fell through. She'd imagined the decor down to the last teacup. Then the bank pulled out of the mortgage arrangement, and another buyer scooped it up. Three weeks later, her husband was unexpectedly laid off. If they'd just bought a house, imagine the financial pressure this couple would have been under! A mortgage would have created a huge strain and would have made finding a new job right away incredibly stressful and rushed. Instead, they spent four months traveling on an extended trip to Asia, using some of the money they would have invested in the home and giving themselves time to figure out their next steps.

Months later, she walked past the flat she'd almost bought and texted me a photo of it, with the caption, "I can't believe I almost had this instead of experiencing Thailand's black-sand beaches!"

Commitment versus Freedom

"Why can't I just be satisfied with things as they are now?" one of my clients asked me over lunch one day. Katie had hired me as a coach to help scale her business, but her dissatisfaction in her personal life was making her palpably confused and upset.

I asked what was bothering her, and she explained that she felt pressured to marry her long-term boyfriend when in truth, marriage was not something she valued. Katie's parents were religious and wanted her to have a traditional wedding — and *soon* — but after talking it out, Katie acknowledged that her parents' values were not her own.

So she and her boyfriend decided against it. They're still together (and happy) but on their own terms. And most important, "everything just feels right about it," as Katie puts it.

A pricey wedding and a commitment that doesn't feel true to your relationship or who you are? No, thanks! Marriage is great for some, but for others — totally the best thing you *never* have, and that's okay!

What do you really, really want? Only you know what's right for your life. If something's not working for you, whether it's a job, a relationship, an investment, a friendship, or a belief that doesn't serve you, dodge that bullet. As Bey sings it, you can find "the good in goodbye."

18

Take Yourself Out to Lunch

*Y*ou're allowed to do something nice for yourself because you want to, not because you've "earned it."

A while back, I started doing this, and I don't tell anyone where I'm going — it's part of the thrill. Treating yourself is a very overlooked way to spend some quality time and congratulate yourself for what you've been doing well.

- Have you been a loyal friend?
- Have you been showing up as a parent or employee, even when you don't feel like it?
- Did you finally let go of a grudge?
- Did you take a risk?
- Have you exercised some courage and done some scary things in order to move forward in your life?

I see you. I celebrate you.

Have a glass of bubbles or aromatic tea, a delicious salad, and say it with me: "[Your first and last name here] — I am so proud of you for ..." Lean back. Enjoy an hour to yourself.

There won't be a better moment in your future to do this — this moment is your *life*!

19

What to Know When You're Not Someone's Cup of Tea

*M*y "I hope this looks intellectual" beige sweater was making my collarbone itch as I sat down opposite a serious, serene-faced nun.

Yep. A nun.

I could hear the rain tap on the glass behind her as she began my interview with the usual niceties. I was an ambitious eighteen-year-old high schooler, and I was being considered for a place at Cambridge University in England. Cambridge is the equivalent of an Ivy League college in the USA. I was *so* psyched to get this far!

"You've already succeeded — no need to be nervous," my supportive high school teachers told me. But I could tell they wanted me to get an offer, not just an interview.

After discussing my grades — which were pretty much identical to everyone else's — my interviewer was curious about all my extracurricular activities. Instead of enjoying lacrosse and learning Latin, I spent my evenings and weekends in a department store selling perfume and at a local restaurant waiting tables. For the record, I genuinely loved doing both. And I told Sister Angela so. I thought I appeared industrious by juggling it all and enjoying it, but she seemed unimpressed.

"Studying at Cambridge is a full-time commitment," she said, her brow furrowed. "Part-time work is not encouraged. Something has to give, and it cannot be your studies."

I replied with a line I thought was smooth as heck — quoted directly from my fave book at the time, *The Magic of Thinking Big*: "Sister Angela, I believe capacity is a state of mind."

Sister Ange frowned. It wasn't what she wanted to hear. I can still feel the cold room and the loud ticking of a grandfather clock interrupting the awkward silence. My sweater, the dry air around us, her response — it all felt a little prickly as she saw my enthusiasm for more than just Shakespeare.

And now, eighteen years later, I still stand by my sweet little line. Because what we can do, and how much we can do, and why we do it *is* up to us (ask my single mama of five girls).

Recalling this experience always makes me smile at teenage me. My dad, who was alive at the time, was beyond amused with my response. "Bloody sure of yourself, aren't you?" he said, smiling with pride.

For the record: I wasn't being rebellious. I was being myself — it gets you all sorts of names. But I was pleased my dad was proud of me. As you have probably guessed, I didn't get a place at Cambridge. The nun didn't want me, and that's okay. She's just one person on a large planet.

This is what I know for sure: no matter what the world thinks about what's impressive and ideal for a person, *it doesn't have to match what you think*. You don't have to contort yourself into being the right fit for a person or a place. I ended up making my gap year to Australia a permanent move, skipping college, and becoming a career woman younger than expected (which to me was the goal of college, right? To set you up for career success?). Sister Ange's rejection of me was perfect, then. Amen.

20

Stop Trying to "Balance" Everything

*T*he ocean has peaks and troughs. Even if you've been rowing along in a steady boat and the water has been still for ages, sometimes a big wave will come out of nowhere and just knock you right on your butt.

What do you do when an unexpected wave hits you?

You change position. You might have to stand differently — legs apart, arms out. You pause what you were doing and just adapt to the new, temporary wave. You wait. The calm will come back eventually, and you can't argue with the waves! They're different every day.

How does this apply to life on steady ground?

Well...

If you've recently had a baby, *this is not your time for balance.*

If you just lost your job and need time to process the change while reaching out to your network and seeing what opportunities are out there, *this is not your time for balance.*

If you're sick, moving, dealing with grief, or processing any big life change, *this is not your time for balance.*

"Balance" becomes problematic when we believe we need it in every situation and at all times. We don't.

It can be a wellness trap and a buzzword that's more pressurizing than it is helpful. No, thank you very much. Give yourself room to not be balanced while the waves are rocky, and don't waste a single second thinking it has to be different. All extreme weather conditions are temporary. You can be where you are without resistance. Life is as dynamic as all its elements.

21

Everyone Has (Invisible) Scars

*H*eath is a great skier, and when we were dating, I noticed a scar above his knee. "Skiing accident," he said. "I went off piste and…" (I'll spare you the gory details of the bone protrusion). He was proudly displaying his courage as a skier, believing in his abilities and in going off course.

Why can't we be equally as proud of our emotional scars?

Because I'm a coach, a lot of people open up to me about their life, and sooner or later, they share the things that have caused them pain — but not physical pain. More like a divorce, something someone said that cut deeply, or a failed business venture.

These are your invisible scars. You can't see them, but they're a mark that's been left on you. We all have them if we've lived a few years. We've all experienced some struggles. No one gets through life without *some degree* of scarring.

I like to reframe what having a few scars — the ones that only we see — really means. It's not the physical scars we get from sports, accidents, or the oven (in my case!) but the unseen ones that we hold close and perceive as bad.

The only way to experience a scar-free life is to lie on a bed of cotton wool until you die. Screw that!

So what do your scars prove to you?

First, they are evidence of where you've been and are unrelated to where you're going. Second, they show that you took a risk! You're courageous! What risk did you take? Living in a new city? Working in a new industry? Believing a marriage would work out? It's better to be in the game of life — actually living it — than "safe," watching on the sidelines or repeating the bunny slopes day after day. You don't regret-proof your life by doing nothing. *You live regret-free by taking chances.*

The fact that you did something — whatever it is — that resulted in a wound means that you let optimism rule over fear. You had the courage to dance with the unknown. Every parent, entrepreneur, and human welcoming progress and change understands courage. And that deserves credit, not criticism.

Rock your scars; they're evidence that you're living your *life!* Like any bold skier, you were brave, too. In a different way.

Notice that people who fail to risk anything love to voice their opinions about your scars. They love to tell you what was a good or bad idea in your past. Let them … they can stay on the sidelines! A lifetime on the bunny slopes is boring as heck.

22

See the World in High Definition

Some things are allowed to be *just* for you and not your social media (even though some days I know, I know, you just can't help yourselfie)!

I adopted this thought after I heard a rock climber say the best views he gets when he reaches each summit he breathes in for himself, versus whipping out his phone. It's like a small, gorgeous, even rebellious-feeling act of self-love.

And hey — *the best things in life aren't Instagrammable.* Think about it. A funny confession shared over a burger and an iced tea with your best friend. A long-standing inside joke with your partner. A quiet walk. The sunset or ocean anywhere (not even the best filters beat the real deal).

Ever notice how you have so few pics with your family and closest pals? There's value in not sharing some experiences. It can be delicious to hold back and enjoy some things privately. Letting your pasta go cold as you helicopter over it with your phone is just *a bit sad*. (Breathe in the garlicky aroma instead — lean in and lift that fork!)

The best, most consistent, and *really real stuff* can't be captured on any camera. It's something that can only be felt within.

And if social media (or traditional media like the news) bothers you, you can — without apology or explanation — sign off. Tune it out. Hey, what you don't see can't bother you. Any habit you're not changing, you're choosing.

You won't miss anything. You're not late in returning a DM from the queen of England. And if anything really, *really* important happens (like a hurricane is heading your way or a celebrity couple splits), someone will call you.

23

A Little Extra
Makes All the Difference

*W*hen everything went virtual due to the COVID-19 lockdown, I found a Spanish tutor online. Her name is Silvia, and she's just splendid — we spend 30 percent of the time laughing. Once, I asked her (in semicomprehensible Spanish) how long she's been teaching online.

"Not long," she answered. "I actually work at the university, but it's closed in Mexico City, so this is a little extra work for me!"

An hour or so later that day, as I folded clothes out of the dryer, I named each item to myself in Spanish — *falda* (skirt), *camisa* (T-shirt), *calcetines* (socks). And I thought about sweet Silvia and how appreciative I am that she decided to go for that *little extra* work.

It made me think. Isn't success defined by that "little extra"? It's not the dramatic, far-reaching, overly impressive actions or risks we take that push us forward. It's simpler than that. It's the extra showing up. The extra giving to others. The extra learning. The extra reps, even, during a workout.

This is what, over time, makes the difference in our life and in our contributions. Ask any expert at anything, and they'll agree. There's nothing mystical about having a big, generous life. It's just about the willingness to do, give, and become *just a little bit more.*

I paused while folding a warm *camisa* for a second and thought that a "little extra," in fact, can add up to a whole lot.

And then I thought, *Where has this been true for me?*

- When I first moved to New York in a recession with no job or college degree, I worked on my confidence every day ... *a little extra.*
- I get into a lot of the media I love because I do my research and follow up ... *that little bit extra.*
- I have close, lasting friendships because I call and stay in touch with my pals ... *extra!*
- When I started out as a life coach, I knew I wanted the side hustle I was rockin' to be *big.* So I gave it *extra everything* ... and I'm now running my full-time business (the best thing in my life after Heath!) in its eighth year.

Let me ask you: *Where can you give a little extra? Where do you want to?*

24

Be Easy about Sex

A friend of mine was complaining recently that in her five-year marriage, her sex life has really slowed down.

"That's okay! It happens! These things can come in waves," I said. Followed by, "What are you going to do to get it goin'?"

"Well," she answered, frown forming, "I was googling sex therapists. And then I went down a rabbit hole about what could be wrong with us. I mean, it could be my recent exhaustion from work or that I don't make the effort to dress up enough, and well, I did gain a bit of weight in the last year, which makes me feel..."

"Stop!" I said, perhaps a little too abruptly — hand signal and all.

It was a true *let it be easy* moment.

Anyone who has been in a long-term relationship has or probably will come up against intimacy gaps at some point. Freaking out is not the answer. Nor is diving deeply into "the problem."

I shared my gentle suggestions, which have worked for me and countless friends over the years:

Think loving, sexy thoughts toward your partner. Look at them through the eyes of someone who might spot them across the room at a party. Remind yourself why you were attracted to them in the first place. Just because someone is familiar doesn't mean you can't foster a fresh attraction. It's up to you and your thinking! Passion (and orgasms) begin in the mind.

Physically touch your partner. Do so in a romantic way that doesn't have to lead to sex. When was the last time you had a long, lasting kiss? Or a hug that lingered for more than two seconds?

Stop making your partner "wrong." My friend Alexandra, an intimacy expert, taught me this important lesson: *someone who is wrong all the time is not sexy at all!* When we criticize our partner nonstop, we become less attracted to them. How can a person who is wrong all the time seem sexy to you?

You're allowed to disagree without anyone being wrong — for example, if your partner refuses to get into the plant-based meat substitutes you're loving, validate your partner's side of things. "I like veggie burgers, but I respect your midwestern carnivore side!"

A wrong person doesn't feel sexy or attractive, to you or to themselves. So stop trying to win fights. It's killing both of your sex drives.

You can also ...

Ask questions! Instead of jumping into conflict as a reflex, use it as a chance to get to know each other better. For example, instead of saying, "You're too stingy with money when it comes to eating out!" Ask, "What are you saving for? Tell me what you want in the future."

Being open-minded fosters closeness and intimacy, allowing you to understand your partner in a whole new way.

Choose curiosity over judgment. Instead of using critical language such as saying something is bad/boring/dumb/annoying, be curious instead. "This isn't a TV show I'd normally watch, but I see you love it — what's so good about it?"

Bonus relationship hack. Whatever you're telling your partner helps shape what they become. Your life partner is your biggest decision and most important teammate — so be on their side! You reap the benefits, too.

There's an old joke I love: "A husband and wife are driving around in their hometown, where he is the mayor. They stop to get some gas, whereupon the wife recognizes the station attendant as a high-school boyfriend. After they drive off, her husband tells her, smugly, "See, if you'd married him, you'd be working at a gas station." The wife replies, "If I'd married him, he'd be the mayor."

Touch, respect, admiration, and building each other up — these are all sexy behaviors that will bring you much more closeness than focusing on problems. You don't need new lingerie or Botox to increase intimacy. Your emotional connection enhances your physical connection — they're entwined.

25

Argue for Your Possibilities

*I*f you argue for your limitations, you get to keep them. But if you argue for your possibilities, they expand.

We are experts at knowing our limitations. We defend them doggedly. We set up Judge Judy–style courtrooms in our heads and play the part of the prosecution — against ourselves. Against our own possibilities.

What if we flipped the script?

Next time you're about to prove a personal limitation, pause. Is it helpful, to you or anyone else? I've never found it to be so.

Are you "too sensitive"? Maybe you're highly empathetic, and that's a superpower!

Are you "disorganized"? Maybe you're an action taker who focuses on the overall mission over tidy perfection.

Are you "on the bossy side"? Maybe you're a natural, confident leader.

What's there to apologize for or explain away, exactly, here?

Here's a fun exercise. Imagine you're responsible for defending your possibilities in a courtroom. If you had to be your own attorney for just five minutes, what would you say about who you really are and what you can do?

26

Just Decide

*N*ineteenth-century Austrian poet Karl Kraus said, "A weak man has doubts before his decision; a strong man has them afterwards."

Make decisions. When you know, you know. And that's easy enough, right? But what about when you don't know? You decide. Clarity doesn't come from overthinking. Or asking everyone within earshot what you should do. Or polling your peers.

Get quiet for a minute. You know more than you think you do. Indecision is not always about not knowing what to do. It's about not trusting ourselves. Confidence comes from the Latin word *confidere*, meaning "to trust." And trust is built over time, via our own follow-through.

Clarity and confidence come from taking action. A lot of decisions don't even have to be permanent. But we don't have perspective on the situation when we're beating ourselves up over our hesitation.

Can you be a little easier about the next step?

27

Know Your Blind Spots

*W*hen I was seven, I knew a girl who choked on a hard candy, and to this day, I still avoid hard candies. Ever since, I've had it hardwired that hard candy can kill you. Honestly, it's such a pity because I really love Werther's Originals.

This is a tiny illustration of a large truth most of us live by called "the proof by example" fallacy. It means that we derive conclusions from one or a few examples. It's warped, but we all do it.

Now, skipping hard candy is no big deal — but have you written something off forever that could matter? What might you be missing out on?

Maybe you're like me. You're from a small town, and the one wealthy person you knew wasn't very kind to people. So you might think wealth and kindness don't coexist (when, in fact, many wealthy people actually do a lot of good).

Or a friend of yours has a small kid who screamed a lot in the park one day and you think, *That's what life with kids is like. I couldn't do it unless I invested heavily in earplugs.*

Or you know someone with insomnia who started taking CBD oil and it helps her sleep. So now you're convinced CBD oil is the only aid for insomnia.

Some of these biases are more significant than others. But giving into all-or-nothing thinking and overgeneralization massively limits us!

I read about someone who gave up her cushy job to go all in on a nonprofit she was passionate about. And I thought, *Oh man, I'd love to do something like that and just move to another part of the world but I can't right now so....* It would be easy here to think I can do nothing and just close my laptop and turn on Netflix. Instead, I found her nonprofit online and made a donation. Because we can almost always do something small.

Keep those peepers (and your heart and mind) open. An open mind leads to a bigger life.

28

Confidence Is Simply a Willingness to Feel Uncomfortable

*T*his is one of the most important lessons I've ever learned. When it sinks in, it's like you have the secret to the universe within you.

A confident person isn't special, born that way, or unusually good at things. A confident person is simply willing to experience rejection, embarrassment, criticism, failure, or humiliation (or any other emotion that scares us). Most people aren't willing. We are wired to *avoid pain* far more than *gain pleasure*.

What's the worst that could happen if you put yourself on the line by doing something new, scary, or intimidating? *A feeling*. A temporary, bad feeling. It will not kill you or even hurt you. Research reveals that human emotions last for a whopping ninety seconds before changing shape. Ninety seconds! We have more than fourteen hundred minutes in a day, so I think we could all withstand almost anything for one and a half of them.

Like clouds passing in the sky — every shifting and changing shape — all emotions are temporary. Good and bad. The confident person knows that the cost of going for it is therefore worth it. Because what's the risk, really? Experiencing some temporary uncomfortable emotions is as bad as it gets.

What would you be doing if you were willing to experience a negative emotion? Asking someone out, positioning yourself for a raise at work, putting your hat into the ring for a cool opportunity?

You feel nervous asking someone out because of the possibility of rejection. I get it. But you can't find love if you don't take a risk, right? So by risking a temporary, fleeting emotion, you might gain something you really, really want! That payoff is more than worth it.

Life is limitless and thrilling when you can be easier about experiencing some negative emotions. Think about it. Is your goal or your sensitivity driving you? In a few months (weeks, even!) from now, will you be prouder of yourself for leaning toward comfort or discomfort? What will reap a bigger reward for you? Way to regret-proof your life!

29

The Past Does Not Create the Present

$\mathcal{T}$he principle of causality — aka cause and effect — has been studied by philosophers since Aristotle and is a subject explored in metaphysics. It's an abstraction about how the world works and is used in disciplines ranging from physics to theology. It's often used in traditional psychology, too. But here I'd like to offer something a little more empowering.

The basic concept of cause and effect is simple: this action happened (cause) so this is the necessary result (effect).

For example:

My parents had a bad divorce, so I'm unable to have faith in marriage.

I didn't go to college, so I can't be successful.

I went to school for finance, so I can have a career only in the banking sector.

Mom and Aunt Kathy are both overweight, so genetics are why I can't have the body I want. What's the point in trying?

Are these facts? They can kinda feel like they are, right?

But what if we questioned whether or not the principle of

cause and effect holds up in these cases? Most people never, ever question their beliefs. Once you start, you'll realize the superpowers you have within you.

Think about it. If the traditional cause-and-effect model always worked — with the cause really creating the result — *every person with your past would then have a similar, if not identical, future.*

No one with divorced parents would be happily married.

No one without a college degree would have career or business success. (I don't have a degree, by the way, and had a pretty nice corporate career before starting my business.)

No one would have a career unrelated to their education.

Everyone with overweight parents would also be overweight.

The "facts" we believe in crumble here, don't they? Sometimes our beliefs protect us, though. Which is why we lean into them.

If you subconsciously believe in cause and effect this way, you have a plethora of fair-sounding reasons for why you don't have what you want and don't have to change anything. You don't have to be vulnerable with potential suitors because it won't work out anyway. You can justifiably stay in your current job and avoid stretching yourself. You don't have to reach out and network with others to break into new fields or embark on something significant for your health.

Consider a belief you have about an area you don't feel confident in — your education, your relationships, your body. Can you question it? It takes courage, I know. But it's where your confidence and freedom lie! Your mind is your motor, and your beliefs determine all the decisions you make.

Knowing that the past doesn't create the present might make you the most free and powerful person you know. All your power lies in the present moment. Wow!

30

Desire Is the Greatest Force
in Human Nature

I was coaching a well-known influencer one morning and, not long into our convo, I became even more excited than she was about how successful her new product was going to be. To be fair, this is a fairly common occurrence — I am pretty well-known for being high-energy, and I can out-excite even the most enthusiastic folks.

I could see her future. And we were in this high, magical vibe of *Oh yes, and also x! And don't forget y! Wait, what about adding z?*

I live for these moments! Was it her big following, her vision, her competence that made her so confident in her success? Those things can be helpful, certainly. But *something else* drives success.

Just one thing, in fact: *desire.*

I said to Heath straightaway, "She's gonna hit the big-time with her online offer, I know it."

"Why?" he asked. He's more of a skeptic — we've seen lots of people fail and give up.

"Because she really wants it," I told him.

No one can give it to you. And if you have a desire, you have a gift, because, as Deepak Chopra says, "Inherent in every desire is the mechanics of its fulfillment." Fulfilling your desire is what you were made for, right? If I work with a person who has zero following or experience but a deep desire, we can go places together, fast.

And I'll coach a person with desire over a "qualified," well-known, established, fill-in-all-the-fancy-things-here, semipassionate person any day. Because life has taught us that when it comes to winning at anything, lukewarm is just *no good*.

Desire is the best, most energized, and tireless driver on earth. It makes life worth showing up for.

You don't choose your desires. They're built in. Your job is to remove your resistance to them and then have fun allowing them to unfold.

31

Grief Is Love

*T*he Argentinian poet Antonio Porchia said, "Man, when he does not grieve, hardly exists."

I lost my dad to addiction when I was nineteen. When it happened, I was in shock, even though we knew it was a long time coming. Nothing prepares you for news that's so... final.

Anyone who loves a drug or alcohol addict knows the rollercoaster ride you experience alongside them. And the constant fear you live in about losing them.

And still. When death happens, you're never ready for it.

"I feel so abandoned," I said to my mum. Everyone else I knew at that age still had their dad — some of my friends who are twenty years older than I am still do. I have pangs of envy when I see friends, even strangers, with their fathers. I expect I always will, a little bit. No matter how old I get.

My mom said one thing that I've always remembered. And I repeat it when I meet someone else in the throes of grief: "Grief is a privilege. Because love is a privilege."

"You loved your dad and you suffer because your love can't be expressed in the way you're used to anymore."

And without love, there can be no grief.

Grief is proof of love.

How lucky we are to grieve.

32

Every Silver Lining Has a Cloud
(and That's Okay)

I've lived away from my family since I was eighteen. I see them sporadically, and a weird thing happens every time I do. When my sister Liz came to see me in New York and I met her at JFK, the second I hugged her and smelled her familiar, fresh Herbal Essences shampoo scent, I felt a sadness I immediately wanted to fight. She'd just arrived, and already I felt a pang of sorrow! This was the arrivals area, not the departures!

Do you ever feel sadness over goodbyes before they even happen? I sure do. I start to think, *I'm going to be so sad when we're back at the airport again in a few days.*

I used to lament this feeling and try to eradicate it fast so I could just feel better and be *fully in the moment.* But I've started to accept the fact that the sad feeling can actually coexist with the fun I'm having. It's proof of how special it is. You've got to feel it to heal it! And there's nothing wrong with sad feelings.

I'm reminded of one of my favorite quotes of all time from Aesop: "Sorrow is always the twin sister of joy."

If you didn't care about someone, you wouldn't miss them when they leave.

If you didn't have a wonderful vacation, you wouldn't feel a tinge of unhappiness that it's coming to an end.

If you didn't grow so much in a past job, you wouldn't have pangs of nostalgia for it.

It's okay! Life is a series of contrasts. We need the sorrow to appreciate the joy. And remember: the universe is generating plenty more joyful moments for you all the time. All. The. Time.

Bring on the sorrow, then. Resisting it will do nothing for you and in fact can make it worse. This is a great example of *choosing* how you think about an experience. Sadness is an experience, but how you think about that experience determines how you use it and whether it leaves you feeling open and expansive or shut down and withdrawn.

It's all right. Every silver lining has a cloud.

33

Let People Know
You're Happy to See Them

I introduced a friend of mine to a podcast host she looks up to when we all happened to be having lunch at the same restaurant, at different tables. But when I told the podcaster afterward that my friend was a fan, she said, "Really? She didn't seem that enthusiastic to meet me!"

Almost everyone wants to be liked and approved of. They want to fit in. They don't want to come across as a creepy *fangirl*. This can lead to us being edgy, anxious, and even performative when interacting with people. Or like my friend, we can play it *too* cool. But there's no payoff for this. There's nothing wrong with you if you're just a cool cucumber, but other people might not know how you feel about them — and that can be a missed opportunity to enjoy a spark right off the bat.

Know that other people are feeling what you're feeling — even the people we look up to. The best way to cure social anxiety is to help reduce it for others. Give what you want to get! Here's how:

1. **Be enthusiastic** when saying hello to someone! Let them know that you're happy to meet or see them! My friend Adam once recorded a video of me in a little dance as I saw him crossing the street to join me at a restaurant. I know because his boyfriend told me; Adam had texted it to him. You don't have to go that far — but let the people in your life feel your excitement at spending time with them.

2. **Ask questions** about the person you're with. This is the best way to be an excellent conversationalist! People feel at ease once you get them to open up. Focus on anything you have in common, too — where you grew up, people you both know, a TV show you like, whatever. This creates an immediate connection, because all similarities put us at ease. It's called the halo effect: if we have one thing in common, we believe we have much in common. It bonds us.

Enjoy the fun of being generous and making social situations easier with these two simple steps. And watch your social interactions blossom.

34

The Next Time Someone Gives
You a Weird Look

I was having breakfast with a small group of new friends by the beach one morning. We were talking, laughing, and enjoying some true Miami Beach fare: avocado toast, acai bowls, and coffee. As I took a bite of the toast, a chunk of a tooth at the back of my mouth came out. Gulp.

I didn't know these folks very well and so swiftly excused myself to observe the new hole in my mouth (gah)! I came back from the restroom feeling oddly queasy, made a polite excuse to leave, and left cash on the table. A root canal and a couple of days later, I received a text from one of my new friends:

"Hey, everything okay? I hope I didn't say something wrong over breakfast. I was bummed you left early. Xx"

How sweet of her, I thought. In that moment, I was also reminded of the tendency we have to blame ourselves when someone behaves oddly. She thought I was *mad* at her. The truth is, I couldn't even remember what she was talking about after the I-just-lost-a-chunk-of-tooth-and-want-to-throw-up incident.

My only thought at the time had been, *God help me, I have to get out of here!* It's never a good time to lose a piece of a tooth, but one of the worst times has to be when you're around people you don't know very well.

So the next time someone leaves early, doesn't text back, doesn't respond to your funny comment, or whatever it is that allows you to think you have done something wrong — *you probably haven't.*

There are a million weird little things (like broken teeth) going on in every human life. Don't be so quick to worry, panic, or assume *you* messed up.

And when in doubt, ask! When we ask, we lose often silly, self-harming assumptions. My new friend *did* ask, and I appreciated that she reached out. I now know her well and she knows the truth, and we laughed our asses off when I told her what really happened.

(Oh. And unless you have an extremely solid set of pearly whites, *please avoid extra-well-done toast.*)

35

Good and Bad,
You'll Get Used to It!

*O*ur brains host a little-known trap that we're not conscious of, but it's important to know about it. It's called "hedonic adaptation."

Let me explain.

My first job paid me $28,000. Then I got a promotion to $35,000. I thought I was the highest roller in town — for a day or two.

Over the course of my corporate career, I then earned $50K, then $100K, and eventually $500K/year. None of which seemed terribly impressive anymore after a few months in my new salary bracket. Very quickly, human beings become used to each new standard of living and want *more*. Psychologists call this hedonic adaptation. Basically, that's a fancy way of saying that we get used to our life changes *very* quickly. Way quicker than we think.

Don't even get me started on the iPhone upgrades we seek every five minutes because we get used to the most recent upgrade within twenty-four hours — a classic HA trap (I called hedonic adaptation "HA" because it *is* hilarious when you consider it).

Using income as the example here, you know that as you earn more, the stakes are raised each time. And every time our income is increased, taking us from one economic bracket to another, we find ourselves at the bottom of a new rung on the ladder once again. We never feel we've fully "made it" because we are either new to a certain bracket or comfortable within our current one ... or focused on the *next* bracket.

Interestingly, this works in the reverse, too. Many bad things won't make you suffer as much as you anticipate they might. You might fear losing your job for years, and then one day you do — and then you find something else pretty soon. Or you downsize to a smaller home and end up just as happy as you were with one or two fewer bedrooms.

We're highly adaptable and resilient beings.

Bottom line:

New and better things won't make you happier (for long).

Worse things won't make you suffer as much as you anticipate they might.

Because we get used to change more readily than we think.

The only antidote to hedonic adaptation is radical appreciation. *Conscious* radical appreciation. Pay attention to everything you have, the stuff that goes right, all the parts of your life you don't need to complain about. The areas and people and components of your life that don't bother you. I'd bet any amount of money that you're way better off and more blessed than you realize. What would the you of a year ago say about the you of today? Are you appreciating yourself and your many blessings enough?

36

If You Don't Feel Like an Imposter, Are You Really Going for It?

*I*mposter syndrome (or "IS," as I call it) is what we experience when we feel we've fooled others into thinking we're capable when we don't fully believe it ourselves. For instance, you might be a lawyer with ten years' experience under your belt, but you don't feel qualified to speak at a certain conference. Or if you're in line for a promotion that you've earned, you might convince yourself that it's just a fluke that you're being considered.

To be totally honest, I have IS constantly! As in, *all the time.*

IS shows up whenever we attribute our achievements to blind luck or good timing. Our inability to accept our gifts means that we often feel like a fraud and that we might be exposed. It's very uncomfortable.

Most common in high-achieving women, IS not only prevents us from enjoying success, but it also massively limits our potential. Feeling undeserving and fake, we turn down wonderful new opportunities and creative ideas. Imposter syndrome is the killer of many "what-might-have-beens."

Does that sound like you?

Have you ever said you're "not ready" to take the next step?

Or to move to a new city you've long dreamed about?

Or to start an entrepreneurial venture?

Or to apply for a role at a prestigious company?

The truth is, *we're never ready*. It's a myth that "ready" even exists! Being ready is a decision, not a position.

Those who get what they want in this world proceed anyway. It can also feel quite thrilling once you commit to *just going for it*. I've never felt more alive than when I have moved to different countries, quit jobs, and launched entrepreneurial projects.

If I don't have imposter syndrome on some level *all* the time, I know I'm probably coasting a bit. So I've come to regard my sweet little pal IS as a sign that I'm truly going for it! Feeling like a fraud can be a positive indication of forward motion.

IS can make us feel scared and miserable and unsafe, yes. But it can make you feel alive, too. Being a courageous, confident human means a *lot* of discomfort (yes, that word again)! And hey — it's okay! Everyone else is right there with you.

I see you. I know the sick feeling and the "what if?" insomnia and the pull to just stay in bed and shut out the world. Some days it wins, and you do stay in bed. And that's okay, too.

But other days, you push through. Imposter syndrome is there, but it's not making the decisions. The real you is.

37

If They Gossip to You, They'll Gossip about You

A couple of years ago, I was on the hunt for a new designer to help me with some website updates and marketing materials. I met a promising designer, Jo, right off the bat. We had lattes and fruit salads at an Upper West Side café as she looked at my site and shared some cool ideas with me.

I liked her, and in true *let it be easy* form, I figured I'd hire her. *I don't even need to interview anyone else*, I thought. *Saweet!*

As I got the check, Jo mentioned an influencer to me whom I'd heard of but didn't know personally.

"I did her site, too. And her social media graphics," Jo told me.

Cool! I thought. *I've seen her stuff, and I dig it! This deal is so sealed.*

"She's weird, Susie!" Jo continued, and my heart sank a little.

"She's not chill like you. She has freak-outs and sends me Slack messages late at night. She's not like the person she presents online."

I actually stopped hearing the words after that. I felt a swift, sucky pit in my stomach. She was totally talking shit about another client, to a prospective client! *Is this how she might talk about me one day?*

I knew that, talented as this designer was, I wouldn't feel totally at ease with her on my team. I'd feel next in line to be gossiped about if I ever sent a late-night Slack message. So I didn't hire her.

Gossiping can feel good for a hot minute, right? You bond. You laugh. You might find some temporary relief from your own suffering while shining a light on others' issues. But then you can have what I sometimes refer to as a "gossip hangover."

You feel bad. Your lower self had too much airtime (we all have a lower self — that's okay). You feel guilty and ashamed. You have regret. Criticizing someone else's relationship, career, looks, or income doesn't improve yours. The payoff just isn't there. Think about it for a sec. What do you get out of it, really?

Plus, you start to distrust the friends you gossip with, maybe just subconsciously. And they start to distrust you. And rightly so. You may never have noticed this before. But the people who *never* gossip, those who never chime in with a mean-spirited word or comment — we trust them. We feel safe with them. We love them in a different way. Heck, we hire them.

Gossip adds nothing to your life. There is nothing in it for you.

38

Call on Your Imaginary Mentors

I love Sara Blakely. Even before I interviewed her for *Marie Claire*, I was in awe of the billionaire SPANX founder. Sara isn't just a megawatt business genius. She's real and relatable. She doesn't take life too seriously. Most important, she has a ton of *fun*! She's also a natural blonde, like me (*wink*).

But in that interview, she also taught me lessons that I recall often. I was side-hustling and growing my coaching business when I heard her speak these words, which resonated with me:

The importance of trusting yourself and your own rear end is what's going to keep you going. Recognize that failure or the word *no* is not the end. *No* wasn't even something that registered for me.

When I started SPANX, I got my first really big order from Neiman Marcus. You get that big order, and you think you've arrived, but that's when the hardest work happens. I went out and bought all my own products off the shelves and paid all my friends to go buy the SPANX products, because I was relying on myself to ensure success.

I didn't even want to rely on the sales associates in the stores. This was my big break, so I took two years and stood in the department stores and sold SPANX myself, and I felt like, "It is up to me to make sure this happens."

As a human being obsessed with living and teaching self-reliance, I could have wept at her example of self-reliance and action. You are a soul on a mission. The universe needs your hands, your voice, your tenacity, and your courage to create. This interview was a divine experience for me.

Now, I don't have a WWSD (What Would Sara Do?) bracelet or tattoo, and I don't have her on speed dial (yet)! But when I have a challenge, a setback, a problem, a flurry of self-doubt, I often think, *What would Sara say about this?*

When you ask, the answers come. Sara always tells me, *"Onward! Next! You're doing great! Believe in yourself! Stay the course!"*

Keep a mental picture of your hero close. They give the best encouragement.

And if you keep listening and taking action, maybe you'll be the imaginary hero called on by people just like you and me ... sooner than you think.

39

Stop Saying, "I'm Proud of You"

g love to praise! I live for it. Typically, if there's anything nice to say, I want to say it all. Like, every nice word ever.

And then I started to have mixed feelings about it for some reason because it started to feel, I don't know, a little...cheap, maybe? People who barely knew me would tell me, "I'm so proud of you!" I knew they meant well, but isn't that something a parent, life partner, or mentor should say, because they invested in you and the pride is warranted?

It's not a big deal. It just feels a little — inauthentic?

Then I came across psychotherapist Alfred Adler's model for praising better, which he simply calls "encouragement." Adler said that when we simply *praise* someone, giving them compliments like, "You're so smart" or "You're so attractive," we create a *vertical relationship*. In that moment, we become the judge of someone else's intelligence or beauty.

But when we simply share that person's impact *on us*, we foster a *horizontal relationship*. An equal relationship. So instead of saying, "You're so smart," you might say, "When I'm with you I always learn new things." Or instead of telling my friends, "I'm proud of you," I'll say, "I'm proud to know you" or "I'm proud to call you a friend."

Here's why: even a good judgment is *still a judgment*. But our personal experience of a person or thing is ours alone. I started weaving this practice into my life, and it just feels more real.

Here's an example:

Your friend Amy helps you organize your home. She transforms it from cluttered to chic, and you're amazed.

Praise: "You're an organizational whiz, Amy! You're such a pro!"

Encouragement: "Amy, you really helped me today. Thank you. Before you came over, I felt overwhelmed. Now I feel calm and different, and I love my home in a new way. I appreciate that so much."

Can you feel the difference?

If you must use the word *proud*, a more encouraging way to say it could be, "You must be so proud of yourself." That way, it's self-validating, not externally validating.

If you want your compliment/feedback/love to land more deeply, then remember — encouragement is more real than praise. It's easier, too. There are no perfect words to find, just the truth from your heart to express.

40

The Best Coaching Question Ever

*W*hen we feel powerless, it's because we feel like we're out of options — even when the feeling is subconscious. But what we don't realize is that there are *always* options. When you are reminded of this fact, you begin to feel powerful again. Like a job candidate with three offers, the more options you have, the more powerful and in control of your future you feel.

Let me tell you now. You have the equivalent of three job offers.

Unhappy in your relationship?

Assuming your relationship is a healthy, nonabusive one, you can:

- Decide to accept and love your partner exactly as they are. It takes only one person to improve a relationship (you — with different thinking).
- Leave.
- Go to therapy.

Unhappy at work?

- Start a side hustle and create a plan to quit.
- Update your LinkedIn profile and ask everyone in your network if they know about any openings.
- See if there are opportunities you can uncover at work in order to improve your job. Might there be some you haven't noticed yet?

Is your best friend toxic?

- Make new friends. Get out more. Remember that plate from before? The one we filled up with lots of healthy greens and good-for-us activities and people and ideas? Fill up your plate with more people who are good for you!
- Have an honest, loving conversation with your friend about how you feel, and be prepared for any outcome.
- Allow them to be who they are and just spend less time together!

Ask yourself: *What do I have control over right now?*

It's an excellent question because the second you ask it, your clever brain comes up with options on demand. Let this question interrupt all your most worrisome thoughts.

We are so ready to give away our power. Why? We forget our options. We forget what we have control over.

Shoulders back, sunshine. You're more in control than you think.

41

The Grass Is Greener
Because It's Fake

*W*ho or what are you comparing yourself to?

I used to envy a self-help author who seemed to have it all: a big audience, cool clothes, a chic life, nice family, and multiple homes. And then someone who knew her well told me, "You know she has serious food issues, right? She was in the hospital last year."

I didn't know that. It was also apparently no secret. Her spiritual work was an effort to heal herself. I didn't see that — I just saw the sweet-smelling, bright-green country-club grass she was seemingly living on. It looked perfect. And mine looked *just okay* next to hers. But I was focusing a lot on the bald spots on my lawn...and had never stopped to consider that hers might have some, too.

I've had plenty of issues of my own. Like shame stemming from growing up in a poor family and a background with addiction and domestic violence. However, I've never had significant issues with food. As soon as I heard about this author's troubles, I was reminded of the illusion of perfection we project onto others. (I recently heard that she's doing great, by the way, and as I understand it, her work has helped her heal her relationship with food as much as it has helped her followers.)

When we think someone else has it all, we see their lives in only one dimension. The truth is, *everyone struggles.* As author Regina Brett says, "If we all threw our problems in a pile and saw everyone else's, we'd grab ours back."

But we look only at their green-ass grass and compare it to our bald spots. It's not a fair side-by-side comparison, and it never can be, because we'll never know the full truth about other people's lives.

The grass is greener because it's fake. Not the grass itself, but the lens through which we see it. It's distorted. Here's the key to peace: *Tend to your own grass.* The grass is greener where you water it. Someone else out there envies something about your life without your even knowing it. Envy yourself.

42

Stop Picturing Success
(and Do This Instead)

*T*he coaching world used to be so bro-y. Don't get me wrong, bros can be fun and can have good ideas. But success consists of much more than this hypermasculinized approach. There are different strokes for different folks and as many metrics of success as there are humans out there. The whole super-bro, "Eff yeah! I got your million-dollar secret right here!" vision turns me off. What can I say? The idea of buying (*cough* leasing) a Lamborghini or hanging out on a private jet with a bunch of chilly-looking nineteen-year-old models isn't exactly motivating for me.

But that's what the bros were selling — what one image of success *looks like*. A question I prefer to ask is, What does success *feel like*? Poet E. E. Cummings said it beautifully: "Whenever you think or you believe or you know, you're a lot of other people: but the moment you feel, you're nobody-but-yourself."

How you feel is only known and understood by you. Success to me feels expansive, peaceful, calm, and self-assured. It's not about being flashy or dominant or frantically signing up to every new social media app that pops up and attending every event out of FOMO (fear of missing out). Been there, done both — you're missing nothing.

What something "looks like" is really about self-image. You're really asking, *How does the world see me?* But what something "feels like" is about self-esteem. *Am I valuing myself and what's true to me?*

Feel, feel, feel your way into your next right move. It's incredible what the mind can do when the heart is giving the instructions.

43

When You Thrive, Everyone Wins

I repeat this to everyone who is scared of reaching a new level in their life. They think, what will people say when I ...

Pay off my house?

Start a business?

Take a trip around the world?

Write a book?

Show up as my real, honest self on social media?

The answer is, inside they'll say, "Look at that!"

Whenever we do something that feels new or hard or scary, we are showing other people what's possible for them, too. My friend Lizzie, who is a nervous driver and sticks to the same seven or eight routes (school pickups, runs to the grocery store, visits to her parents' house), decided to drive two hours during the pandemic to help a relative. She was terrified, but her desire to help won over her fear. She was scared, but she made it there and back (slowly ... but who cares)?

It turns out that her older relative is also a nervous driver. But when she saw Lizzie do it, she returned the favor and drove out of her way to help another person a couple of weeks later. Lizzie showed her that new roads were possible — literally and metaphorically!

The same goes for anything courageous we do: paying off debt, falling in love after heartbreak, giving up alcohol, starting a business with no experience or training. We become real-life examples of what can be done. By anyone.

Living a small life is not inspiring or helpful to others. Sometimes we're mistaken about this. We think if we shine brightly, it might make other people feel bad. That may happen, too, but the real message brought by success is a generous one.

Your prosperity helps others prosper. Yes, some may be intimidated, but most will be inspired.

It says: Hey! Look what you can do, too.

Grab your keys.

44

The Oscar Curse Is Real

*H*ave you heard of the Oscar curse? The idea is that many actors' lives are plagued after they win the coveted golden statuette. Their careers take a dive. They get divorced. They develop substance-abuse issues or get in trouble with the law.

This is connected to a popular self-help theory: self-sabotage is most common when life is at its best. In *The Big Leap*, author Gay Hendricks calls this the "upper-limit problem." It means we hit an upper limit of what we'll allow to be good. We make life hard. We won't let all the good flow. We won't *let it be easy* by letting the good in.

I mean, are we *allowed* to thrive in all areas — health, wealth, love, adventure — when many people aren't?

Yes.

It's not "too much good"?

No. No!

Next time life is going swimmingly for you, bringing with it a wave of discomfort or quiet anxiety about how long it will last, ask yourself, *How much love/success/happiness am I willing to let myself experience?*

This upper-limit problem has manifested in my life more than once, but now that I am aware of it, I can see it more clearly. When my business is going great, I realize that I tend to initiate fights with Heath. Whenever I get great news, I tend to overindulge in online shopping. On one birthday some close friends came to visit me in Miami, and we were at their lovely hotel pool. They surprised me with key lime pie (my *fave!*) and sang "Happy Birthday." The day was perfect, but I just had this feeling of foreboding like, I just couldn't let all the joy in. It was as if there was too much happiness and my heart couldn't contain it.

Maybe you recognize that familiar feeling of "This is too good to be true — it can't last!" and the pull to bring yourself back to what feels familiar instead, like having at least one problem to manage (at all times). It's like we all have a set point of a "I'm allowed to feel this good" instead of a "I'm allowed to feel fabulous."

I try to identify my self-sabotaging tendencies as evidence of things going right in my life. This can provide a huge sense of relief!

Where can you increase your happiness tolerance right now? What part of your life can benefit from your kicking off the artificial lid of how good things are allowed to be?

45

Pain Is Good
Because It Makes You Move

*H*eath has had back pain for years. As an athletic person, he lived with it by just sucking it up. It was only after the pain became too extreme to bear, following a run one day, that he sought out the chiropractic help that made a difference.

I liked my corporate job until, after years, I felt more and more depleted and less and less energized. I also had three shitty bosses in a row. So I started a side hustle! My journey as a coach and columnist started when I knew there had to be another way.

My best friend was in an emotionally abusive, on-and-off relationship for years. Only when she and her partner had a screaming fight in a car park — where she felt physically threatened — did she say goodbye for good.

"Enough" is a powerful feeling. It stirs action and change. The universe makes us miserable sometimes in order to make us move. Where are you miserable right now? What is it telling you?

Do you need to suffer longer before you make a change and do something? Your inner wisdom dials up the volume right on cue. *Listen up, buttercup.* Something important and new could be revealing itself to you. The life force that sustains us all is wise. Maybe something is being made hard so that it can transform into something easier for you.

Enough, is.

46

Commitment Makes Life Easy:
The 100 Percent Rule

I have a friend who quit eating sugar a while back. When we go out to eat, I almost always get dessert. "Will you have a bite?" I ask, testing her. "No, thanks!" she always responds, with ease and indifference. Must be so hard for her to turn down a bite of chocolate mousse every single time — right?

Wrong.

Put simply, it's far too easy to waste our time, money, and energy by not committing *wholeheartedly* to something that's important to us. We intend to start a blog (for real this time) but keep getting distracted by social media. We try to cut down on shopping in order to save for a big purchase like a house but end up spending way too much money on clothes or going out to eat.

Our well-meaning "99 percent effort" is exhausting. It consumes energy without producing results. It's stressful. It makes us feel like a failure when we're not — we just haven't gone all in yet.

Putting 99 percent effort into things that matter means we fall short of our potential — and feel bad about it. When my business was beginning to take off, I attended a conference where I heard a statement that I knew would change everything:

Ninety-nine percent is hard — 100 percent is easy. Or as best-selling author Jack Canfield puts it (in slightly more aggressive terms!): *"99 percent is a b*tch. 100 percent is a breeze."*

Take a moment to let that sink in.

It seems counterintuitive, right? Stick with me here.

Consider the following individuals: my sister, a strict vegan; my neighbor, a six-time *New York Times* bestselling author; and a comedian who publishes a new YouTube video every week without fail, no exceptions or excuses.

Are these things hard? Maybe they were when these folks first got started. But now my sister knows exactly which foods to buy, where to buy them, and how to cook them. The author writes every single day, not just when he feels inspired. The YouTuber is constantly learning new skills, researching, and developing new routines, each one better than the last.

If something is tugging at you and has been over time, you've probably been "99-percenting" it for too long. Here are three steps to help you 100-percent it instead.

1. **Identify exactly what needs your 100 percent.** Your writing? Your photography? A business idea that's been percolating for a while? A habit you need to quit altogether — online shopping, hanging out with a toxic person, drinking soda or alcohol? Not everything in your life needs 100 percent effort. But your intuition knows what does. You don't have to go crazy and commit to a million projects or banish pleasure from your life. Your

100 percent right now is probably just one thing. What is it?

2. **Take action.** Commit to writing for one hour a day, seven days a week. Pinpoint exactly how to make your first sale for your business (you can do it)! Delete your online shopping accounts, end that relationship once and for all, throw out the soda or pinot noir. You have full permission not to look back. (I did this with alcohol after my thirty-seventh birthday, and the ease and joy of it surprised me!)

   I hit 100 percent mode when I write books. It's not easy, but it's easier than thinking about my book on the way to meet a friend for lunch, on vacation, when cooking, and when scrolling Instagram.

   Ninety-nine-percenting is hard. It weighs on you daily. It's heavier than the actual task at hand. The decision fatigue is crippling: "Should I write or go out?" "Should I write or go grocery shopping?" "Should I write or call a friend?" When you shift gears to 100 percent, there are no more decisions to make. It's write or die!

3. **Repeat (again and again).** When we apply the 100 percent rule to a task at hand, we complete it. A project gets wrapped. A once-hopeful intention becomes a habit. A goal is met.

Adequate mental space is then freed up for the next priority to become clear, since we don't have the brain fog or guilt about other unfinished projects. And when we give 100 percent, other not-as-important stuff just falls away. It's an awesome perk to an already pretty awesome rule. People respect you for it, too. You have clear boundaries. That's something to be proud of.

Why do some people succeed more than others? Because they commit. If you know anyone who is self-made and grew their wealth over time, you know they are not 99-percenting their investment strategy. If someone writes bestselling book after bestselling book, you know they're not sitting down to write when inspiration hits (that's a bonus!) or whenever they feel like it. If you know someone who's built up a loyal YouTube following, you know they're continually making the effort to put out unique content. Commitment is ease.

47

Loving You Is the Real You

*H*aving an enemy feels off, doesn't it? It feels heavy. Uncomfortable. Not good.

Let me share a story I heard about Leonardo da Vinci. Some children were watching him paint, and one accidentally knocked over his canvas. Da Vinci was angered and kicked the kids out of his studio. He picked up his brush to resume his painting, only to find that he couldn't do it. He had been trying to paint the face of Jesus. But he couldn't do it with anger in his heart.

When there is anger, irritation, any negative emotion in your life, you block the flow of creativity to you. You cut yourself off from vitality and freedom, because anger or hate cannot coexist with love and everything good that flows with it. Releasing your anger and frustration is a huge gift you give yourself. For this reason, I try to find positive qualities in the people I don't like and to forgive the people who've hurt me (with boundaries, of course — it's not like we hang out). Not liking someone activates your shadow self, and not much good comes from that, for long.

In *A Course in Miracles*, it says, "Only love is real — everything else is an illusion." Like our friend da Vinci, we don't want to buy into what isn't real for long because it blocks us up. When you experience nonloving emotions, that's a sign that your ego is having a field day. And the feelings might feel fair and justified in the moment, but they won't feel good for long or reap any real rewards. Because your inner guidance wants you to return to your true nature — which is love. That's why loving someone feels so good (it's hard to argue with that, right)?

PS. The same block appears when you are angry or annoyed at yourself. A self-compassionate lens might not be your default setting, but you still deserve it.

48

When You Think You're Not
[Fill in the Blank] Enough

*I*f you think you're not fast enough, not pretty enough, not interesting enough, not whatever you're believing right now enough, ask, *Who made me?*

It wasn't you.

Hey, you didn't create you! Don't argue with the creator, eh? Do you want to argue with the divine intelligence who created all things — dolphins, mountains, stars, puppies, sunsets, the sweet smell of fresh grass, and a billion unique snowflakes? The same creator made you, including your strengths, talents, capacity for joy, inner wisdom, body type, natural passion, height...

You're equipped with everything you need to fulfill your potential. Maybe you weren't born with supermodel looks or family money or connections. Me either. So what?

We don't need them. Use what you've got! It's perfect. Just accepting this and getting busy will take you far.

There is *nothing* to gain by arguing for your perceived

limitations, not even for a second. Rock what you've got! If you pretended, for just a few days, that exactly what you have is enough, what would you do first? It can be priority numero uno on your get-to-do list.

49

The Best Thoughts Ignite
This One Feeling

*W*hat do you spend your days thinking about? How can you tell if your thoughts are serving you? By how you feel when you're thinking them! This is real-time, foolproof data that never misses.

Thoughts create our emotions, which create our actions, which in turn create our life.

What does this mean? It means our thoughts matter more than anything else — because they, in fact, create our life. The good news? We can *consciously choose* our thoughts. We can opt for the thoughts that feel good. And our body is so perfect that it can tell us when we need a thought redirect. Our negative emotions are like a neon sign flashing within saying, "Thought upgrade please, thought upgrade please!"

Sucky feeling? Thought change needed!

How perfect is that built-in system?

Because our emotions are real-time data about what we are thinking, we can actively employ a thought-replacement technique.

We often think euphoria or excitement are the best emotions. To be fair, they're pretty fun, yes. But it's even simpler than that.

You know that feeling when you wake up from a nightmare and realize that the unthinkable has *not* happened? Relief. Or when you're certain you've lost your wallet and you find it stuck between the sofa cushions? Relief. Or when you think you hit "reply all" on a company-wide email — and you didn't? Relief.

Well, you can create this relief for yourself, all the time. Think — what's a more soothing thought than the one you're thinking right now? This strategy will transform your *life*! Here are some examples:

If you're thinking: *This meeting will be terrible; I will embarrass myself in front of my boss.*

Try instead: *Maybe I'll be a bit anxious, but I can cope with that if it happens, and it might not happen. I was okay last week at that other meeting.*

If you're thinking: *I am not good at this, it's hard.*

Try instead: *Everything is hard before it's easy. I am learning as I go, and it's not my job to be perfect!*

If you're thinking: *I'm so nervous heading to this party where I don't know anyone and I have to make small talk.*

Try instead: *Most people are a bit nervous at social events! I always feel anxious for the first few minutes, but then I usually end up enjoying myself. I can always leave whenever I want.*

Relief thoughts are all *let it be easy* thoughts. You can always create one, at any time, no matter what. Isn't that amazing?

Something that is causing you stress can change with just one thing — a new thought! Thought upgrades even make your body and behavior change. Your shoulders relax, your breathing is deeper, you're nicer to people. Try it and see!

50

What Palm Trees Teach Us
about Resilience

*L*iving in Miami, I've always been in awe of the palm trees here. (I'm from the UK, and I can assure you, there is not a single palm tree in that gorgeous land. We have other strengths, like perfect pub lunches and quaint villages.)

I marvel at the palms that now line my street. They're magical. To me they scream, "I'm on holiday!" and "This is the place to be!" And then I learned something about my favorite trees that made me fall even deeper in love with them.

Have you ever noticed how palm trees bend in hurricanes and storms but don't break? In fierce winds, the palm tree moves, bows, arches but remains standing. It's flexible.

This alone is remarkable — flexibility equals survival, after all! But wait... there's more. A native Miamian I know told me that when heavy winds hit palm trees, the roots actually stretch. *They grow stronger. The storms that hit these trees actually strengthen them.*

When I look at the storms I've weathered, I think of the roots they gave me. I've stretched, bowed, waited out the weather — and come back to myself a little stronger. This is true for you, too.

This knowledge helps makes all the storms a little less scary when they come.

51

What You're Not Changing,
You're Choosing

*H*eath and I decided to leave New York, our beloved home of ten years, over happy-hour crostini on a random Tuesday.

"Okay!" I said when he asked if I was ready. This was after a few months of Heath encouraging a move to a place with a more relaxed pace and a warmer climate.

Two months after our crostini conversation, we were sipping coffee on our sun-drenched terrace in Miami.

It seemed so fast to everyone else. But not to us. What's there to wait for? Decision-making is really just trusting in yourself. We don't have to be so serious about every decision that pops up, and ultimately, we need to stop being so hard on ourselves for the "bad" choices in our past. I think of it in terms of wanted or unwanted outcomes instead of "good" and "bad decisions." And most decisions are reversible anyway. This makes driving a big change in your life so much easier.

Mundane decisions can be made easier by having a plan: fig-ure out your outfits, meals, and calendar ahead of time. Batch your decision-making, even! For example, for sixty minutes every Sunday evening, you meal plan for the week. If you can learn to take care of certain tasks ahead of time, you can save time, and stress.

Bigger decisions just require getting quiet with yourself and tuning in to your intuition. It feels wild, but it's also wise. Logic has a place in the world, yes: we can do the numbers, consider the options and the outcomes, and weigh the pros and cons until Christmas. But the most important decisions in life are seized by instinct. We feel them. That's why confident decision-making is so commonly referred to as "listening to your gut."

Logic isn't everything — and it never can be. To make good choices, you must trust your inner voice. If you don't feel intuitively guided, that just means you are not fully aligned with yourself in the present moment. Maybe you're stressed-out, overtired, or overthinking. That's okay, too. (You might just need some quiet time, a walk outside, or more sleep.)

Inaction *is* action. Meaning, if you don't move to Puerto Rico, forge ahead for that VP title, start a side hustle this year, or call off your less-than-satisfactory relationship, you are *deciding* to live in Chicago. You are *deciding* to remain in your job. You are *deciding* to reject entrepreneurship (and more dough). You are *deciding* to stay in an unhappy relationship. What you're not *changing*, you're *choosing*!

If you sense a big decision looming in your life, don't hide from it! That makes it worse. Consider your options — there are at least three in every situation. Then get back to that gut!

Line up fully with your decision. Fall in love with it. That's a decision you get to make, too (and a really good one).

52

Fun Is Always an Option
(Even When Things Go Wrong)

"*O*oh, I'll pack a couple of jackets and some pants!"
I was excited to pack my carry-on to see my mama in England during one extra-hot Florida summer. I honestly love the Miami warmth but was excited to go home and visit my mom in the UK, where it's considerably more pleasant to walk and sit outside in August, when it usually stays in the mid-60s or so.

And then I arrived in England — just in time for *a record-breaking heat wave.* This was a serious one, complete with constant weather warnings and nonstop news updates across the country. Anyone who's lived in or even visited the UK during a hot period knows that it's not set up for über-warm temps — there's no AC in homes or on public transport, and there are few fans around. It's just not a place that typically gets hot!

So … what then?

We had fun anyway.

Yep, even with my seventy-eight-year-old mama who was adamant about staying indoors in her small apartment with the curtains drawn. What else could we do? Complain? Well, then you'd be missing the point of your life. *Fun is an option*, even when you don't think it is. No matter where you are or what's going on or how unexpected the weather is.

So we sat together on my mom's small sofa. One overused, dust-covered, small fan juddered as it twisted its little face back and forth between us. We talked about life. We listened to each other's stories. My mum read the first draft of my book. We sipped tea. We kept putting the kettle back on. We learned some Spanish together on the Duolingo app. ("Technology — incredible!" my wide-eyed mum exclaimed in her thick Polish accent.) We laughed as I showed her good, clean, funny Instagram memes that I knew she'd like the irony of.

Another time, I was in a long line at Party City around Halloween. I watched a young couple joking around for the entire twenty minutes or so. Everyone else was looking annoyed and huffy with the holdup. I heard the young man say to his girlfriend, "You'd be that balloon," as he pointed to a witch. They burst out laughing, and the back and forth of who-would be-what-balloon continued the whole time they waited. I even giggled quietly to myself (trying not to appear as an eavesdropping creep). They probably had more fun in that slow-moving line than some couples have on their honeymoon.

I mean, why let a rainy day ruin your beach trip when you could be playing Scrabble and making out with your partner instead? Fun is always an option.

53

Don't Rob Yourself
of New Experiences

I'm lucky that I get to meet a lot of clever people who can imagine and understand something conceptually — without ever actually experiencing it.

I have one clever friend who says stuff like this all the time:

"Oh, yes! You pitch the media and get on TV — makes sense!"

"You started a coaching business by one-on-one coaching and then creating programs that could serve thousands of people at once! That's good to know."

"Success is simply a series of small wins over time? How logical!"

It's wonderful when you feel seen and heard by people who can know — or try to understand — your experiences. But.

Knowing is not experiencing.

Don't cheat yourself out of experiences. They are what create the rich tapestry of your life. Experience, good or bad, also makes you magnanimous without your even knowing it.

You can see the world via Pinterest images or via your own senses.

You can watch a hero's journey in a ton of different movies or forge ahead on your own quest.

You can admire others for quitting a job to pursue their dreams or take the risk with your own resignation letter and twelve-month plan.

And once you learn, you're able to share, teach, and show up for others in a bold, authentic way. Experiences connect us. Experience more. It's never wasted. Live, don't just observe, life!

54

We Are Everything
We See and Feel

*W*hat do you love, admire, or look up to in others? *It's your light being reflected back at you.*

Annoyed, mad, or frustrated at someone? *They're reflecting back at you something you don't like about yourself.*

Everyone reflects your light and shadows back. We all have both. Writer Anaïs Nin put it succinctly: "We don't see the world as it is, we see it as we are." It's a courageous act to acknowledge this.

That person you look up to? It's you. You couldn't revere someone unless you matched them in some way. The person driving you crazy? They're revealing a part of you that you'd like to transform or a part of you that needs healing. (That's all a trigger is — a negative charge revealing something within you that needs some love.) Who is revealing something to you right now? Good or bad, it's a gift to know yourself more intimately.

55

The World Will Always
Match Your Energy

I was feeling stuck and uneasy at work one morning. I didn't love my job. The VP was stressed-out (I could hear her strained tone on a conference call in the next room). The office had a tense vibe all the time, and I couldn't bear the thought of spending seven more anxious hours in my cubicle that day. I wanted to rest my head on the table and wait the rest of the day out, alone.

Enter Anika.

Anika was visiting from the London office and strutted in wearing a cute linen dress and Ray-Bans and holding an iced Starbucks. "New York, New York!" she beamed. "Sun's out, fun's out — where will we go for lunch today, Susie?"

And just like that, my mood lifted. Her upbeat spirit elevated me (and I'm pretty certain other people in the office, too).

Your energy matters. It impacts others. Because it's powerful. Are you entering a room or a conversation from a defensive perspective or an open-minded one? I heard that Oprah Winfrey put a sign in her dressing room that said, "Please take responsibility for the energy you bring into this space."

Other people will match your energy. Are you thinking loving thoughts toward your partner while you're on your road trip? Or irritated ones? The person you love will pick up on what you're putting out there and reflect that same feeling back to you. If you're anything like me, it's easy to forget this. We can spot it in other people but not in ourselves as readily. If my energy is really off one day, I prefer just to lay low for the benefit of everyone.

Whatever energy you bring to a situation is going to set the mood for your interactions. Peace will always begin right there within you. Be lovingly responsible for it.

56

Saving Money Is
Expensive Sometimes

*T*here's an Aesop fable that I repeat over and over again — in
business and in life. It goes like this:

> *A poor widow had one solitary sheep. At shearing time,*
> *wishing to take his fleece and to avoid expense, she sheared*
> *him herself but used the shears so unskillfully that with the*
> *fleece she sheared the flesh.*
>
> *The sheep, writhing in pain, said, "Why do you hurt me*
> *so? What weight can my blood add to the wool? If you want*
> *my flesh, there is the butcher, who will kill me in an instant;*
> *but if you want my fleece and wool, there is the shearer, who*
> *will shear and not hurt me.*

What does this mean for you and me? In an effort to do everything ourselves, we can end up worse off — and so can others.

Where are you skimping in your life, thinking it's for the best?
Are you doing all the housecleaning and missing Saturday mornings with your kids or friends, even though a weekly housekeeper

is well within your budget? Do you take the cheapest flight possible and struggle through fourteen hours to get to a location that you could've made in six for your short vacation (and end up arriving stressed and tired)?

If you're starting a business, are you patching together free information on the internet instead of investing in a course, coach, or mentor who will show you the way — step-by-step?

In life, you pay one of two ways: financially or with your time and energy. You can always make more money, but you don't get more time.

Think: Are you really gaining by skimping on investing in something? Spending is saving sometimes.

57

Just Be on Time

I used to work for a boss who was her own worst enemy. Natalie was a great leader, but her smarts were always undermined by her lack of organization. When the company founders would fly in, she'd be flustered and almost always late to the meetings. One time I waited till the very last second to board a flight with her, and she rushed in, juggling her bags right before the gates closed. I was freaking out that we'd miss the flight and that our multiple meetings that took me ages to set up would be canceled.

I'm a punctual person. I used to think it was because I'm a Capricorn.

I now realize it's because I don't want to go through life anxious and apologetic or unintentionally rude to others. When you're late to any situation, you enter it with an apology. Don't willingly do that to yourself. Be on time and see how relaxed it feels and how everyone apologizes to you because *they're* late! Being punctual is an easy way to display that you've got your act together. It also shows respect to others. You can't always control it (especially if you live in LA and you have to drive!), but a lot of the time, you can.

And if you are more than a couple of minutes late, you don't have to explain to everyone why (no one cares about the intricacies of the traffic on I-95). Just say, "I'm late — apologies!" and move on.

58

Don't Underestimate
Your Contribution

*I*t took a lawsuit to help me understand my worth.

My first career was as a recruiter. One time, a client didn't want to pay the placement fee for a young woman I placed in his real estate firm as a sales assistant. As a young people-pleaser, I was very conflicted. My client didn't want to pay us because the new hire wanted to leave after a few months (she told me it was because of his too-intense management style).

My boss insisted that he must honor our agreement — I mean, I had done my job, but it just hadn't worked out. But I still wanted everyone to be happy. And I felt sick being in the middle. In the end, I had to side with the agreement my client had signed in ink. He owed us the fee. But I still felt responsible (and really bad for him).

Until.

The legal firm that represented us made me share *all* my work on the recruitment project, plus all my correspondence. My meetings with the client. More than a hundred emails. Job ads written and paid for in the local newspaper (oh, those sweet older times). The many interviews I conducted with potential candidates. The multiple reference and background checks. Second interviews I coordinated. Third.

I handed over a hefty chunk of paperwork and thought, *oh, wow.* I did a *lot* for this client, who expected me to do it for free. It took hours of combing through everything, and the subsequent paper trail hit my boss's desk with a *thud*, which punctuated with perfect clarity my resolve on the matter: "I will never underestimate my contributions again."

This was my first real understanding of imposter syndrome — even though I didn't have the language for it back then.

I allowed myself to go through this mental loop: "Well, this job is fun and I love people, so maybe I don't have to be paid for every single job placement because I enjoy the work so much."

Just because work is fun and easy doesn't mean it's not worthy of great compensation. You're better, smarter, and more valuable than you think. You don't need a court ruling to tell you this (I won, by the way).

59

Boredom Is Dangerous

uthor Steven Pressfield once said that if we overcame our resistance to our life's work, hospital and jail cells would all be empty. He calls our procrastinating, waiting, hoping — our general inability to just sit down and get the work done on anything that matters to us — *resistance*.

Resistance is dangerous. We experience waves of boredom while resisting, too (easily soothed by getting into the waste-of-time social media scroll-hole)!

What are you putting off? Where is boredom showing up in your life?

Boredom is dangerous because our minds love momentum. We want to think, create, innovate, do, engage. When we do nothing — unless we're doing so consciously, as in meditation — we can get into a scroll-hole of our own that *doesn't even require a phone*. We think of past problems, mess-ups that could happen in the future, and how we've failed.

"Idle hands are the devil's workshop," as it says in Proverbs.

When was the last time you were busy *and* feeling down?

I was watching a cooking show recently. The cooks have forty-five minutes to create a perfect dish that could rival that of a famous chef. In those forty-five minutes, no one is concerned with anything but the job at hand. The time disappears, and there is only space for focus (and yummy outcomes).

When I separated from my first husband, my therapist advised me to stay busy. He was right. I said yes to every invitation I got for a year. Who has time to look back and rue the past when you're going on road trips and to art evenings, tango classes, and barbecues?

Hey — we need opportunities to find our talents! Engaging in life supports this. "Get out more" is generally pretty great advice.

We're happier when we're busy. We're *happiest* when we're *progressing*. This is not advice to overload your calendar. It's a reminder to engage in stuff that keeps you focused on what you want. The next time you feel low and resistant and restless, ask yourself, *What's a fun way to fill my time?* Don't overthink it. Get busy!

60

It's All Relative

I was speaking to my sister in Switzerland during the month of December.

"How's the weather?" she asked.

"Cold," I said. At 61°F (16°C), it was sweater weather in Miami.

"You?" I asked back.

"Ah, warm here! It's lovely."

I asked the temperature. It was 57°F (14°C).

What does this tell you? No one sees the world in the same way. We view the world around us based on context and timing and the points of view that each human being has accumulated throughout their life.

What are you going to do — believe that someone else's interpretation is wrong? There's no such thing as cold or warm weather!

We can be *easier*. Live and let others live with their temperature readings (and everything else, for that matter: what a healthy sex life looks like, what's a good use of money, what child-rearing method is best).

The more open you are to the truth being a relative concept, the less threatened you'll feel as you walk through life, too. Because there's not a right or a wrong way to live life. Just like there is no warm or cold weather. There's just people. And the temperature. Nothing to fight against, complain about, or prove right.

Talk about ease.

61

No One Intends to Screw Up Their Life
(a Lesson in Compassion)

*W*hen I was a kid, I sometimes had to clean up my alcoholic father's vomit. He would say, "I'll have a cup of tea tomorrow." (His code for, "I'll stop drinking tomorrow.")

Over the years, I got used to this repetition. Addiction is so frustrating and sad because normally repetition in anything creates progress. But with addiction — no progress. Just suffering.

Eventually, I started going to Al-Anon, which is a program connected to Alcoholics Anonymous but intended for people who are worried about someone with a drinking problem. (I highly recommend going to a meeting if you love someone with an addiction — it's saved many marriages, families, and friendships.)

At one meeting, my leader told me, "There's no law against self-destruction."

The next time you think someone is wasting or ruining their life, remember this: no one wakes up in the morning thinking, *How can I eff up my life today and hurt a lot of people?*

Author Mary Shelley said, "No man chooses evil because it is evil; he only mistakes it for happiness, the good he seeks."

The brain is wired for survival. Our intentions are positive, even when they don't make sense to other people. We're all seeking relief. We all want to feel better. This shows up in different forms for different people. Knowing this can allow us to forgive and be accepting of others.

We all have different ways to cope. This Al-Anon wisdom can save your relationships. It can save your life. It can loosen the grip on the delicate nature of human relationships and help us acknowledge the ways in which we believe we need to control others.

Going easier on other people allows you to be easier on yourself, too. There's nothing to fix. Just people to love. Even when they don't "deserve" it, it's still easier to love. Because love is the only thing that's real.

62

Good Enough, Is

*D*id you know that perfectionism has nothing to do with high standards? It's about failure anxiety.

A perfectionist rarely works at more than 50 percent of their potential. They're afraid to take risks. Afraid to ask for help. Afraid to get it wrong. The common theme? *Fear.*

What if good enough actually *is* good enough? The most prolific, high-producing, creative, and successful people I know have a big bias toward action. They aim for excellence, not perfection (which doesn't exist, anyway).

And they reap more. There's a Spanish proverb, "More grows in the garden than the gardener knows he has planted."

Reaping is for the planters, even messy planters. I think to myself, *If this piece of work, meal, outfit, whatever, is an 8 out of 10, that's good enough!*

Better a burgeoning, boppin', wild, alive backyard than the perfectly coiffed rose garden that never blooms.

63

Tell People Who Are Suffering They Are Not Alone

*B*efore I learned how to *let it be easy*, I was hard on everyone — including Heath (mostly Heath). I would be annoyed when he was late, when he stayed out too long with friends, and even when he wanted to sleep in on the weekends (what a treat I was)!

After less than a year of marriage, Heath wanted to leave. I noticed that he was withdrawn, tired, and stressed-out. I saw that he was pulling away and thought, *What does he need?* He was stressed-out at work and home, and I could only imagine that he felt alone and sad. Feeling alone itself is sad.

I wrote him a card that read:

I know that you are sad and things are hard for you right now. Just know that you are not alone.
I love you.
Xo

Heath still has the card. It's the only card he's ever kept over the years (and I'm a big giver of handwritten notes)!

Tell people who are suffering they are not alone — and then just be there for them, even in silence. Presence and attention are both love. And it's enough.

64

Couples Therapy — Just Do It

*H*eath and I have been to couples therapy three times in our marriage. Once it was about sharing our money (we decided to, in the end). The other two times we just found each other unbearable and uncompromising. Walking into Howard's office on the Upper West Side of New York City, I said, "Heath can't just have a job and that's it. He needs to side-hustle like me — and help me out more!"

Then we would sit for an hour on his comfy sofa, as his dog Phoenix tried to sniff Heath's crotch, which brought some levity to the otherwise tense room. (Thanks, Phoenix.)

At that point in our lives, I had a full-time job and a thriving side hustle as a coach and columnist. I could not believe my husband (or anyone, for that matter) could be okay with doing just one thing. (I cringe at past me for being so pushy — and frankly, impossible.)

Howard said, "Susie, you couldn't be with someone as high

intensity as you, someone who is go-go-go all the time — you two would *combust*! Heath's even-keel nature is important for you."

And then he said to Heath, "Susie pushes you because she pushes herself. Appreciate how industrious she is and the life she's creating for you both!"

It's like we had never seen each other and our relationship in that way before.

Howard asked a great question each time we came back to him: *"What would you most like the other person to know right now?"*

You can ask your partner this the next time you can feel a fight coming.

I'll say now, "I would like you to know that I'm tired and over-whelmed with ..." and Heath will say, "I would like you to know that I need some help in this area ..."

Communication. Simple yet hard sometimes. Therapy — and even this one question — helps it be easier.

Divorce is more expensive than therapy. Just go!

65

Unmute Yourself

*B*ritish literary critic John Churton Collins said, "If we knew each other's secrets, what comforts we should find."

Several years ago, I was dealing with anxiety, which manifested as a big desire to control everything and become angry when I couldn't. I took some medication for it — but I didn't tell anyone. Until.

I noticed that a close friend.at work had anxiety that was palpable, and I told her. Another friend's husband had spontaneous angry outbursts when things didn't go his way — and I told them both. I met a stranger on a train who told me she has permanent, low-level anxiety all day, every day. I told her.

I was not giving advice. I was just sharing something I did that worked for me. No matter what someone else decides to do, it's always helpful for them to know there are options. It's comforting to know that other people feel the way we do, that we're not alone.

And as a human being on planet Earth, I feel it's my obligation to share what has helped me in the small chance that it could help someone else.

Everyone has stuff they don't share, and that's a good thing. It's your life, and your privacy. There's no judgment needed. But sometimes it can be generous to share what feels a bit scary. And to seek out truth tellers, too — for your own comfort.

We can all benefit from knowing that people with beautifully curated Instagram accounts are all just winging it and that they have their own private struggles. They're just trying to make it through the week, too, I promise. (I've coached loads of them.)

66

The Present Moment Creates the Past

"*I*t doesn't matter who my father was. It matters who I remember he was."

This quote from the poet Anne Sexton reminds me of my fantasy TED Talk. (Don't we all have a fantasy TED Talk?) I'm planning to start with something like this:

"A Story of Two Girls: One grew up in shelters, surrounded by addiction, abuse, and uncertainty. Chaos was her almost daily experience and default setting. The other had educated parents, loved school, and felt sure of her parents' love for her. She felt grounded in books and her close relationship with her sister."

They're both...me. So which story do I tell — and most important, which story do I tell *myself*? The one that feels good! They're both true. That's how powerful your brain is — you get to choose!

The present creates the past. You can change your personal story at any moment. Our mind can be our friend or our enemy. We get to write and rewrite the past. We choose our stories. This statement applies not just to the stories we tell ourselves about our parents but to everything else in our past.

Ask any two siblings about their parents and their past, and you might not believe they came from the same family. Or even two people who work at the same company.

Repetition creates our truth. What we focus on and remember expands.

67

Don't Deprive Others
of the Joy of Helping You

One of the most beautiful truths on earth is this: *people want to help you.* Think about a time you helped someone who really appreciated it. How did you feel? Good, right? Allow that for others, too! Just show your gratitude.

We come back to the truth of who we are when we are in service of other people. I'm reminded of this quote by the poet Rabindranath Tagore: "I slept and dreamt that life was joy. I awoke and saw that life was service. I acted and behold, service was joy."

When we don't allow others to help us, it's often because we don't feel worthy. We're happy to give but feel guilty and uncomfortable receiving. And as a result, we rob others of the joy of helping us.

Who can help me?

That's a question I ask now whenever I'm stuck. Heath is always surprised at how quickly I solve problems because I never figure out anything alone if I don't have to.

Asking for help is efficient. Maybe I need creative ideas — and so I'll ask my copywriting friends. Or business advice — I'll ask my entrepreneurial peers. Maybe I need someone to help soothe my anxiety — I call my calm and loving sister. Maybe I need to rant about a situation that feels unfair — I'll call my funny and understanding BFF. Help comes in many forms. Allow it in! See how it bonds you more closely to others. Allow other people to help you, too. They want to! There is pleasure in giving, remember that.

And remember to show up for other people, too! If you don't know how, ask, "How can I best support you right now? I'm here."

68

Putting Yourself First Is Generous

*B*efore I hear you cry that "doing you" is selfish, know this: *what we do to and for ourselves is what we do to and for others.*

Think about it this way. If there is an old, sad, rotting lime in the back of your fridge and you wanna make a gin and tonic with it, is the juice inside going to taste fresh and delicious even though the poor lime has been neglected?

Nope.

What about you? As you show up to make your contribution at work, at home, as a friend, are you fresh and delicious? Or neglected and a bit sad looking?

If you don't take care of yourself, what use are you to others?

How are you feeding yourself internally? Are you nourished? Taken care of?

Acceptance, self-love, and appreciation of yourself allow you to give the same to others. Because we give what we *are*! There are no exceptions.

The starved person has nothing to offer. How can someone stretched thin be authentically generous?

Think for a moment: How do you show up when you are rested, happy, calm? Think of a time when you felt this way. Maybe you're picking up your cousin from the airport as a favor, but you're exhausted and it's your day off. Are you all slow-motion open-arms embrace in the arrivals area? Nope!

Or you said yes when a friend asked you to help with a gala, but you're slammed with work projects or with homeschooling your kids. Are you enthusiastic and energized to find the best floral arrangements? Heck no — you'll say yes to the first vendor you find (two stars on Google? Hey — maybe someone made a mistake)!

We get self-care wrong. We think it's spending a day at the spa or flying first-class, but it can be as easy as stopping after one glass of wine, prioritizing sleep over anything else, or saying no to a client or friend. How do you show up differently when you've been putting yourself first a little?

When things are right with you, they're right with the world! Remember that.

69

A Secret Superpower

*H*eath has an annoying habit of always wanting to do something *just* as I serve dinner. He wants to find a fact in a book. Use the bathroom. Send a quick Slack message. It used to drive me *crazy*.

Now I just start eating and let him join me when he's ready. Sometimes I'll say to myself, "Ah, this is the precise moment I normally get mad and start telling Heath what to do."

That self-reminder is a moment of pure consciousness. It's when we're the observer, not the doer. It's a separation of stimulus (what's going on externally) and response (our reaction).

Conscious thinking, when you can catch your ego before it bubbles up and starts taking over, is a superpower. Can you try it?

Warning — you might feel like Buddha. You'll be unmoved by what's happening around you, like a statue in a noisy, crowded park. It's addictive and powerful. *Om.*

70

Don't Just Consume, Create!

After my last book, *Stop Checking Your Likes*, took off, people started asking me questions like:

How do you strike a balance with checking your social media?
Is there a way to enjoy "likes" in a healthy way instead of being addicted to them?
Do you feel like your online presence makes or breaks your future opportunities?
Do you feel like you "have" to be on social media all the time?
Do other people have to like what you post?
How can you be yourself without being vulnerable and addicted to other people's opinions?

Here's my best tip on how to let social media be easier (and better): Use the fifty-fifty creation-to-consumption ratio — for every twenty minutes spent consuming content, spend the same amount of time *creating* content (a post, stories, a live). That way, you're engaged in the conversation. It's better to post, like, and engage as opposed to just getting caught in up the scroll-hole observing others. Just like interacting with people you care about in person — at a party, for example — can be beneficial, while simply watching others from the sidelines may make you feel worse.

If you ever say or think that you "get sucked in" to social media, don't pretend to be so passive, pet!

No one has a gun to your head. You're powerful and free. And skipping the socials for a few days here and there is good for you and helps remind you that your "inner like button" is the best — when you're easy and allow it to be easy, too.

71

Talk about It, Already

*T*hinking of getting engaged? Or have a friend or relative who is? The following conversational topics can help shed some light on your future together. I wrote an article including these topics for *Marie Claire* in 2014, and I still get letters about it.

As Kahlil Gibran said, "Love does not consist of gazing at each other, but in looking outward together in the same direction." When it comes to these important topics, are you and your future spouse looking in the same direction?

Life priorities. What matters most to you both? Do you want to nest and settle down or go traveling together? Go back to school? Do you want to volunteer in India? Save for a beach house? Talk about your aspirations and objectives, and get comfortable with a relative timeline. Life throws curveballs no matter what — but your plan keeps you on course (and keeps arguments at bay).

Money. How will money — assets, helping family members, paychecks, inherited sums — be handled once you're married?

What happens if one of you loses a job unexpectedly? Being married means you are a team and you need to be on the same financial page, as this is a huge, contentious issue for many couples who divorce. If there was a single thing that separated my first husband and me, it was completely opposing views about money. Harmony on this subject is crucial for long-term unity.

Children. Do you want them? When? How? How many? What values, ideals, and education do you want them to have? Will there be a stay-at-home parent? "Yes, we both want children" is just the starting point!

Workload. This refers to all the unpaid work done at home. How will it be divided? This issue can make for an unpleasant shock if you don't cohabitate before you wed or discuss who will clean the toilets, take out the trash, or vacuum.

Family. Do you envision spending holidays and vacations with your in-laws, siblings, and extended family? Will you see family every weekend? Once a month? Two to three times a year? This can be an especially important conversation if you're an only child (or both of you are).

Elderly parents. What will your physical and financial commitment to them look like? This subject is remarkably easy to overlook. People in their forties and fifties are now referred to as the "sandwich generation," raising children while taking care of aging parents. What will your roles and responsibilities be for your parents and in-laws?

Sexual expectations. Sex while dating or being engaged can be very different from sex with your husband ten years down the road. What would please you both? Can you talk about it in a playful and open way — maybe over dessert one evening? You can take turns saying, "Dream long-term intimacy for me includes …"

If you allow in some potentially uncomfortable conversations earlier on (remember, we're good at being uncomfortable as confident humans!), the clarity only sets you up for more ease later.

72

Stop Fighting with Yourself

$\mathcal{I}$ was reading Louise Hay's book *You Can Heal Your Life* when I
was struck by an idea of hers: she says that we always talk about
"fighting" cancer and often use war language with ourselves and
our bodies in general. We win the fight or we lose the battle. You
hear it all the time. We use "enemy talk" on ourselves more than
we realize.

Louise believes that we create every illness in our body and
that the word *disease* itself means a dis-ease with our body: "Every
cell within your body responds to every single thought you think
and every word you speak." (I also once heard her say that if you
don't believe in the mind-body connection, you've never had a
sexual fantasy.)

The result is that we're fighting with our own bodies, which
feels hard. And yet, all we want is healing and peace, which pro-
vides ease. Fights don't allow ease. We're activating more of what
we don't want.

Thoughts and words are powerful. They impact our cells. Our

thoughts are silent, discreet, and not-to-be-messed-with power-ful. Can we use different, healing language instead? Fighting is exhausting and stressful, not to mention risky. Alongside proper medical care and/or medication when needed, I love these re-placements for "enemy talk." I repeat them to myself whenever I need them (or text them to friends and family when they're not well):

My body knows how to heal itself.
I am strong.
I am supported.

This applies to more than health, too!

A friend of mine said to me over brunch, "I'm sick of fighting for my marriage!"

Instinctively, I said, "Give up the fight, then! Be easy. Tell me what you love about Mike."

She then gushed, over eggs Benedict, about how he's just the most attentive dad, and when she recently had to fast due to a medical issue, he fasted with her because he said it "felt right" to him. Just like that. Weapons down! Ease-ometer up!

It's simple but significant. What language are you using? Battle commands or ease talk? Is the focus on harmony or war? Change your focus and words, and notice the difference immediately.

73

Australian Wisdom
You Can Use Every Day

*I*n Australia, there's a lovely expression you tend to hear multiple times a day. "No worries." It can mean many things:

You're welcome: *all good, sure thing, forget about it, you don't need to thank me,* and *everything is fine.*

Or quite literally: *don't worry.*

What would it be like if you worried a bit less? I love what Esther Hicks says about it: "Worrying is using your imagination to create more of what you do not want."

I used to think worrying was a form of planning. That being worried all the time meant I was being responsible. That if I didn't worry about an event, I wasn't prepared somehow. That's *bonkers.*

I can catastrophize that my husband will get physically hurt somehow...or I can read a book. I can worry about losing my mom, my last living parent...or I can plan a trip to see her. I can worry about something terrible happening to my nephews...or I can clean out my makeup bag.

A friend of mine, a new mom, went to the doctor for a

checkup, and the doctor could tell how anxious she was about being a good parent. The doctor said, "Just feed him and love him, that's all you can do. Don't worry."

A well-directed mind is the wisest, most valuable tool on earth. You're in charge of that gorgeous, more-brilliant-than-any-computer force in your head.

Remember that, will you? Life will happen — good or bad — whether or not you suffer ahead of time. So do what you can to be a responsible grown-up and then … that's it.

The rest will be.

No worries.

74

Success Leaves Clues

*K*nowing what you're supposed to be doing with your life doesn't have to be a huge mystery or treasure hunt. You don't have to be a detective. Look back! *Pay attention.* It's all there! I wrote these seven questions for Oprah.com, and I come back to them time and again when seeking direction:

Seeking inspiration? Break out your favorite notebook and a pen, and spend fifteen minutes journaling about the following:

1. What am I doing when I'm slacking off at work?
2. What blogs and books do I love to read?
3. If I could be anyone for a week, who would it be?
4. What do I feel the least insecure about?
5. What's pure and simple fun for me?
6. What conversational topic never gets boring to me?
7. What kinds of people do I feel most myself with?

When you ponder these questions, is a path clearer to you? Don't overthink it! Let it be, and let it flow easily.

75

How to Give the Perfect Gift

I have the loveliest mother-in-law in town. She's generous and kind, and she is always, always, *always* there for her kids and the people she loves.

A while ago, just before we returned to Australia for a visit, Heath and I had the idea of getting her the same handbag that I own and love. But — as luck would have it — because of the Superbowl in Miami, the road to the designer store was blocked, so we agreed to buy it together with her in Sydney.

When we got to Sydney, we told her our exciting plan.

Immediately, Wendy told us she would be "very uncomfortable" with that gift. She explained to me that the cost of that item was overwhelming and it would have made her sad, not happy. She'd feel uncomfortable wearing it and bad about the money spent on it that could go to something else that felt more practical.

Insistent on gift giving, we asked her what she did want, and she knew. A KitchenAid stand-up mixer! She was over the moon to receive it. Now every few days, I get a delighted text from her about how she's using it in new ways.

I never would have thought to give her a kitchen tool as a present.

When we buy what *we'd* love to receive, not what the other person would love to have, we're setting ourselves up for mixed results. We assume that people value what we value. The other person may be uncomfortable with the gift, and we'll end up confused and disappointed when the reaction isn't what we've hoped for.

You can let gift giving be easier, too!

Instead of assuming, make it easy on everyone: *ask*.

76

You Spot It, You Got It

*O*ne of my sisters is an architect. When we were in Europe together, everywhere we'd walk, she'd say, "Look up!"

The beautiful ornate old buildings are what she sees first. It's what her senses perceive, in high definition. A foodie would notice all the restaurants and the details on the menus. A photographer would notice all the best light and coolest potential camera shots.

Because we see *what we are.*

It might sound simple, but this is one of the greatest truths I've learned. It gives me insight into myself and others.

Beautiful people notice beauty in others.

People who are hurt hurt other people.

If people aren't happy for you, they're not happy for themselves.

It takes one to know one, as the old saying goes. This applies to everything and gives you tremendous insight into yourself and others.

What do you see? What does it reveal to you about you?

77

A Positive Mental Attitude
Can Save a Life

I was the youngest child in my family. After I flew the nest, my mom moved to Zimbabwe to be a "house mother" in an orphanage (the limits of conventional living and age do not apply to my mama). One evening, a nearly skeletal baby was discovered in the woods and brought to the orphanage where my mother worked. The adults in the orphanage suggested calling a priest to deliver the last rites because he appeared to have just hours left to live.

My mom immediately thought, *No, he'll be okay — we can save this baby.*

No one agreed with her. But she fed him milk for days, then weeks, via a syringe. She cared for him around the clock. For two years she raised him and only left when she was forced to because her visa could not be renewed.

Jeremiah is now thirteen, living with his adoptive parents.

My mom regularly sends him letters, toys, and books. After

working with orphans for years, she knows the sensitivity surrounding adoption. She says that to a child, especially one with no knowledge of his birth parents or background, "it can feel like reading a book with the first few pages missing."

She says that adopted children need more than shelter and food. They need to be reassured that they are safe, that their family won't disappear. They need to know that they are special and chosen. Because they are.

Sometimes you will see something that others don't. They don't feel what you feel or have the same stirrings inside them. Your positive thinking is a gift. There's nothing naive or misguided about it. Trust your "possibility thinking." It can literally save a life. Even your own.

78

Your Value Is Not Determined by How Other People Treat You

*T*his is a lesson I wish I had learned coming out of the womb. It's easy to think, *If that cool person likes or approves of me, I'm safe! I'm good here. I'll be okay!*

It doesn't work that way. Your worthiness is fixed, whether or not you like it, whether or not you know it. If you fell off a cliff, the authorities would search for you not because you're verified on Instagram or you filed your taxes on time. *You have a human life —* the odds of you being born as you are about 1 in 400 trillion!

You didn't come off an assembly line. You're unique. You're *you*. There will never be another you. Ever. The deepest part of us knows this.

Even if a $100 bill is ripped, crumpled, or dirty, its value remains the same.

Sit up straight, queen.

79

Someone's Death Does Not
Define Their Life

I once asked my friend Riley what a date tattooed on his arm meant to him. He told me it was the date of his sister's death and then explained that she had died by suicide.

I asked her name, then said, "Tell me about Ruth."

It's important to talk about dead people we've loved — they are a part of us. Initially, Riley explained her drug dependency and troubles, probably because he felt he had to explain her suicide (sometimes we feel it necessary to talk about death in a somber, churchy tone — I used to talk about my dad's death that way, too).

But then he told me how funny, sweet-spirited, and easy to be with she was, and how much of a practical joker she'd been. We laughed when he told me how they'd pull into the McDonalds drive-through and she'd ask for "a pepperoni pizza and their best red wine" (imagine — ha)!

The manner of a death or its timing does not define a life. Ruth lived for twenty-four years. How her life ended was just one act, on one day.

"I should change these numbers to her birthday," Riley said.

80

It's Okay to Break Up
with a Friend

I have a friend who left New York City, moved to the suburbs, and had two kids. She was busy with her family and, naturally, started to have more mom friends filling up her weekends. We began to see each other less over time, but the love stays the same.

Life separates people. Have you ever had a friend with whom you meshed so beautifully for a long time and then, after some time and change, you just didn't seem to occupy the same dimension anymore?

It's hard to explain, and it can make you feel guilty. And even a bit confused. You'd be surprised how often the issue of friendships comes up in my sessions as a life coach. It surfaces in the form of questions like, "I find myself wanting to spend less time with my BFF. Why is that?" or "I just don't wanna do happy hour with my coworkers anymore. Is that okay?"

Why is this kind of dilemma so common among my clients? Because they are people who are making positive changes in their lives. They're starting businesses. They're moving cities, changing their bodies, adopting a new spiritual practice. Whatever it is, it's desired forward motion.

Change begets more change, which can inevitably mean a change in your relationships, too. And hey — that's okay!

Let me ask you this: When you were a kid and joined the tennis team, moved to New Jersey, or joined a new school or church group, did you meet people a little bit more like you? With more in common? And as a result, did you spend more time with them?

The same thing happens whenever you change jobs, become a parent, or pursue a hobby or a side hustle. Life will attract more people like you. And that's a magnetic blessing!

Friendship is about shared experiences and joy, not pressure and shared history. It's about being authentically, fully, deliciously yourself. You don't have to compromise who you are to keep a connection with someone. Your life takes off in new ways when you surround yourself with sincere and genuine energy.

Just because you might be going through a personal shift doesn't mean other people have to come along with you.

If you want to slow down a friendship, just become a little less available. Share less. The process can be gradual and gentle. Cooling down can be healthy, easy, and kind (and in fact, no big deal). It doesn't have to be a serious subject in your life that you worry about. You're stepping off the gas, not abandoning the car.

If you want *out*-out, that's okay, too. I know it hurts. Soothe yourself with the fact that not all relationships are meant to last a lifetime. We mistake the longevity of relationships for their success. Maybe a friend you've outgrown is actually a version of yourself that you've outgrown.

It doesn't mean that your friendship failed, or that it's dead, or even over for good. Just for now, it might be *complete*.

81

Let's Revel in Your Accomplishments for a Second

*W*hy do we have goals? To truly live and stretch and celebrate our lives, right? So why do we so seldom celebrate our victories, however small, when they happen? After we've accomplished one goal, why do we tend to go 100 mph straight onto the next thing, without a single pause? Why not take a moment out for congratulations?

Do you ever allow yourself to just revel in what you've achieved? Try it for three minutes by reviewing the past twelve months and how much ground you've covered. I bet you've done more than you realize, especially if you're a future-focused, high achiever — which you probably are, with this personal-development book in your hands.

Remember that a lot of what you have in your life right now was something you once wished for. Are you seeing it? Are you congratulating yourself for it?

The point of celebrating your achievements isn't just to feel great — although that in itself is a perfect and worthwhile goal.

Celebration also gives you a great diving-off energy (dopamine hit!) for the next cool thing. It's also how *you don't miss out on the good bits of your life*. When you're on a bullet train, do you see the view? Nope. It's all a blur — green and blue just whizzing by. What a pity.

I love to ask this question: "How are you planning to acknowledge yourself for this accomplishment?"

Most people give me blank stares.

Buy yourself flowers or a new coffee mug. Get a massage. Take a weekend trip or an easy day off. Just take a step back from the laptop and say, "Well done, me — I did it!" *Congratulate yourself on a job well done.* What are you working so hard for otherwise, exactly? Celebrate every tiny victory! You'll remind yourself and everyone watching how worthy we all are.

The blur of doing finally becomes a clearer view of your one precious, impermanent life.

Here's another thing to be conscious of. Not all your greatest achievements can be measured. I know a successful CEO who disrupted the tech world, but those who knew him closely were most moved by how he took care of his mother with Alzheimer's. Maybe you're not featured in a magazine or you didn't win an award, but you're steady in times of adversity — which can be far more important. Or you forgave when it was hard, or you moved on from being wronged by somebody with grace. Don't overlook your silent, private achievements, too. Often they're worth the most.

82

Can't Forgive?
That's Understandable

I once got on a long-haul flight with food poisoning. Physically speaking, it was one of the worst experiences of my life. Because the culprit was some weird soup with meat in it, I have never in my life touched soup with meat again. Nearly twenty years later, this remains the case. (Remember those murderous Werther's Originals I mentioned in an earlier chapter? I have some food-distrust issues!)

This habit has some seriously good survival value, evolutionarily speaking. As humans, we survive by knowing what hurt us. And by not repeating it.

But... what if it's not soup? What if it's a human who hurt you? And you love that person?

It's okay to feel scared to trust. But if you've committed to move forward, you must pick up the spoon. Soup may not be worth it, but some people certainly are.

If you need clarity, ask questions. When someone betrays us, disappoints us, and lets us down, this can be an invitation to reach a new level in the relationship. I've seen this happen with couples who survive infidelity. While not every relationship can survive this breach of trust, plenty of couples can successfully move past it, if that's what's right for them.

People make mistakes. But it doesn't mean they get to keep repeating them. If someone continues to behave in a way that they know will hurt you, realize that they're *choosing* to hurt you. That's not okay. And if you let them, you're hurting yourself.

If you want to move on, get the information you need. Ask all the questions. Then — *cut off the subject*. Don't repeat months or years later, "You're the one who ..."

If you want to forgive them, and the person who hurt you is sorry and is committed to not doing it again, you can cut out what happened from your life without cutting out the person.

Just as the person who hurt you can't repeat that action, don't repeat the reminder. Otherwise, *you're* the person who keeps hurting you.

83

There's No Such Thing as Normal

*W*hen I first moved to the United States, I was surprised that in my new office it was common to drink something called a Big Gulp, an extra-large soda you can get from a 7-Eleven. I saw these gigantic sodas everywhere, and I thought there must be a special promotion on them or something!

I grew up with no soda. ("We don't have money to waste on rubbish!" my mum always said.) They still feel like a treat when I drink them.

So.

Drinking sodas bigger than your head. Having two kids. Going into debt to keep up with friends who have more money. Binge-drinking because it's Friday night. Getting and staying married. Eating a sandwich with a fistful of meat piled into it. Celebrating a big win with cake or tequila.

It's fascinating what we perceive as "normal," isn't it? Watch a documentary about a part of the world that's different from yours.

See how other people experience their lives. There's no right or wrong way to drink, eat, celebrate, spend your time … there's no right or wrong way to live your life.

Just because it's familiar doesn't make it good or right or true for you. *You get to decide* what is normal for your life.

84

Take a Stand for the "And"

*M*y friend Cathy Heller says this, and I love it.

You can be a parent *and* a big-time CEO.

You can be intelligent *and* beautiful.

You can be a lawyer *and* a musician.

You can be an awesome parent *and* an awesome stepparent.

You can have a day job, a side hustle, *and* a vacation.

The only limits we have are the limits we make up in our minds. You can do, be, and have it all. Challenges exist whether or not you set limits for yourself on top of them. So why not add more "ands" to your life? Who said you can't? And if someone told you that you can't, why would they be right?

Look for evidence in the world about what's possible. It's there, I assure you. What "ands" do you want to add?

85

The Biggest Manifesting Magnetizer: Appreciation

$\mathcal{H}$ave you ever heard of the reticular activating system (RAS)? It's a collection of nerves at our brain stem that filters out unnecessary information so that we register only the most necessary and important information. Imagine how overloaded you'd be without it, with all the images, sounds, voices, activity, and information your brain receives every single second of the day. You'd drown in information and wouldn't be able to leave the house because you'd feel bombarded at every turn. The RAS allows us to see and focus on what matters most.

It's the reason you think about something and then start seeing and hearing it everywhere — for instance, as soon as you choose a type of car you might want to buy, you start seeing it on roads all over town. Or a place you've just decided you want to visit keeps popping up in magazines, or when you learn a new word, you start hearing it in regular conversation.

My friend recently said, "Since deciding I'm ready to have a

180

baby, I see pregnant women and small kids *everywhere* in New York — have they been here this whole time? I've never noticed them all before!"

Yep. They've been there all along! But your good ol' RAS now clocks what's important to you and shows you more of it. Amazing, right? Forget Insta! We create our own filters, all the time.

The RAS tunes in to what's significant to you — and even validates your beliefs about what's true in the world (*New York is not a kid-friendly city* can switch to *New York is full of kids* all of a sudden when our attention and intention shifts).

Here's how this pairs beautifully with appreciation. When you focus on what's working, what's good, what you love, what things are going right, you just keep seeing more of what's good. And therefore, you'll keep having more and more to appreciate. For example, I was once blissed out with a column I wrote for *Cosmopolitan* magazine that had just been published and I was thinking about what was next. As I walked into my hairdresser's salon, I saw *Miami Magazine* on a swivel chair next to mine. If I weren't in the zone of magazine appreciation, I would've been on my phone instead and missed it. I know it! So what greeted me that day, besides the smell of shampoo? Thanks to the network of neurons that zooms into whatever we're thinking about, another potential media outlet I could pitch! And I did. The reticular activating system activates opportunities in your life!

Appreciation is that joyful, thankful, loving feeling you experience when you've just been given a gift.

When you see the world from the state of appreciation, you

see opportunities you wouldn't otherwise. That's why some people have "all the opportunities." They see them because their lens is focused on feeling good.

We work under the laws of our own consciousness, and proof is everywhere. Try to prove it wrong. You can't. Consciously dwell on what you already have that you hope to receive more of — love from your partner, kindness in the world, unexpected career opportunities. See what happens.

86

Keep Your Network Alive

"*Y*ou're always texting, you know!" my husband often says to me.

When I tell him who it is, different names always pop out of my mouth. "Layla!" "Carrie!" "Zuhair!" "Adrian!"

"Who?" he'll ask.

"You know Adrian — she used to work with Alex!"

"Ah, yes!" he'll say, half-remembering someone he might have met or may have just heard about. Adrian. "How is she?"

"She's fine."

"You're really good at keeping in touch with lots of people," he says.

I love the old line: "Surround yourself with people who would mention your name in a room full of opportunities."

There are people we want to keep in our lives and build relationships with, right? And we want to be one of those people for others, too, right? So it's up to us to take the initiative in tending to our relationships! And keeping our plate loaded with intentional good stuff.

Many people find networking — and keeping their network warm and alive — hard. I get it. It can involve lots of people, communities, time zones, different things that keep us all connected. It's hard to know what to say and how to keep the relationship going. But we can let this be easy, too.

So here's a simple way to do it. Keep a list somewhere (even a mental list) of people you care about, people you want in your future. Text, DM, or send them a one-line email every few weeks or so. Do it when you're in line at Zara or when your computer is rebooting.

Hey Adrian! How are you? Thinking of you. Hope you and your family are well. Looks like you had a fun summer. Any plans to visit Miami? I know the best Cuban sandwich down here, and I know you love those!

Hugs.

Xo

That's it.

The world needs people who stay in touch. Because people are worth it.

The quality of our life is defined by our relationships. Staying in touch is easy to do but also very easy *not* to do. But that's good news! Most people don't do it. You will. And if the people in your life are important to you, you'll be all the happier for it.

87

Pity Is Never Helpful

*W*hen I was little, I had a "big sister." The Big Brother Big Sister Foundation does wonderful work, and I loved my big sister Lee.

As a kid who grew up eating basically nothing but Frosted Flakes, when Lee and her husband cooked me a nice dinner, I didn't like it. I didn't want it or even know how to eat it. (A fork and a spoon for pasta? How would I even do that?) They asked if I wanted something else, and I clocked the box atop the cupboard and said, "Cheerios?"

They glanced at each other, and in that moment I could tell they pitied me. It was the worst feeling.

Many people come to me as a coach seeking help on myriad problems in their lives. And I will only see other human beings in their strength. My friends don't come to me for a big, rambling vent session (by now they know that I don't really make myself available for that). But they do come to me for support and love and humor — to be reminded of their options, strength, wholeness, and capabilities. To flip the script on their perceived limitations.

Pity isn't necessarily loving. It just makes everyone feel worse. Seeing anyone in their wholeness is a gift — because you remind them of the truth of who they are.

88

Divorce Is Not a Big Deal

*O*ooh, did I just say that? Yes. I'm quoting an angel I met at a bus stop back when I was a red-eyed, despondent-looking young thing in my early twenties. This savior stranger asked me if I was okay, and I was too emotional to hold back.

"My marriage. It's not working. My husband won't get the help he needs. He gambles. All our money is gone. I don't see a single way it can work." The words just tumbled out. I had used every ounce of my strength not to ugly-cry in public, but I'd reached the point of no longer caring.

"Ah. Well. I've been divorced twice — it's not a big deal," she answered with a kind smile, her head tilted to the side.

Her bus came. She put her arm around my shoulder, told me I'd be okay, and said goodbye.

It was like a sign from the universe. *Maybe I was gonna be okay!*

She was right, of course, and I *was* okay. Look at the statistics. Is divorce sad, maybe? Sure. But not life-threatening or world-ending. I know that marriage is to be respected and taken seriously. I love being married, and Heath is the most important person in my life. But marriages often don't work out. That's reality. It's okay.

So. What does it mean when something doesn't work out like you'd planned, exactly? It means you had the courage to believe in something. In love. In a future. In the beauty of what could be possible. Heck, what's the alternative here?

I'd rather believe in something that doesn't work out than be a cynical nonbeliever (a truly sad way to live).

The universe loves people with divorce certificates just as much as it loves everyone else.

89

The Secret to Contentment —
Even If You Feel Lonely or Sad or Lost

*H*aving been a bit of a nomad my whole life, I'm pretty comfortable with not having typical holiday celebrations. For example, I got married at city hall with three guests, Heath and I rarely do anything special for our wedding anniversary, and we often spend Christmas on our own. And guess what? I *love* it.

Sure, it would be nice to spend all the end-of-year celebrations with my mum and sisters. But we all live in different countries — my mum's in the UK, and my sisters are scattered around the world. *It's not possible.*

I'd love to play Scrabble with my dad, but he died when I was nineteen. *It's not possible.* Kids are fun to be with (and so is playing Santa!), but Heath and I don't have any. So enjoying Christmas-morning new-toy excitement? *It's not possible.*

Why is my version of doing life good for me? Because of an undramatic — but gorgeous — decision I made a long time ago.

To love what I have.

I swear, this one decision might be the one you'll thank yourself the most for making. Here are a few things of varying importance that all evoke a swell of appreciation within me:

- Miami palm trees
- A husband who I love to eat Shake Shack with and run a business alongside
- Friends who leave me audio messages of songs they're singing
- A new season of a good TV show
- My good health
- Money in the bank because it gives me options
- Money that's no longer in the bank because I donated it
- The choices afforded to me as a woman living in America
- Books
- Access to wisdom
- And most important … power over my mind

What do you have? It's probably a lot more than you think.

I love what I have. I am more than thankful. It's not just enough, it's *beyond* enough. What we focus on expands.

What do you have that makes you feel full of appreciation?

90

Sulking Is Worse Than Fighting

*W*hat's the worst part of fighting with someone? The never-ending you-owe-me-something-now sulk period that can happen afterward, right?

I remember reading about a study of couples who all lived in a house under observation for a month-long period. Relationship experts analyzed who they believed would "go the distance" and stay together long-term. Interestingly, it wasn't those who didn't fight that had the best chance of long-term success. Because conflict is natural. It's bound to happen. It was those who *bounced back quickly* from fights that had the best chance.

My best friend dated a guy she really liked, but if they had a disagreement, he'd sulk for three days. Three days! That's a whole weekend and more! Ain't nobody got time for that. In the end, she said, "His weird silent treatment feels like toxic behavior. I can't do it anymore."

SPANX founder Sara Blakely said that when she and her hubby fight and it gets intense, they slow dance. Heath will try to make me laugh by telling dad jokes or talking to me via the dog: "Why does mum look so mad? She's so pretty! But not with that scowl. Woof."

Sometimes, if we've been silent for ten minutes or more, I'll just go to Heath's office and give him a hug.

Can you snap back faster? You'll add life to your years (and quite possibly years to your life).

91

Just Thirty Minutes Is Enough

*W*ant to write a book? (Heck, even a blog post?!) Work on your art? Create something you've been dreaming of? You do not need two months in the South of France to get it done. Or even any time off at all (although, hey, nice work if you can get it). If you have only thirty minutes to do something creative, those thirty minutes can be potent! As I write this chapter, I have just twenty-five minutes before I need to leave for a meeting. Use the pockets of time you're given. Put your phone under a blanket for half an hour, and *create*)!

It adds up. As the Buddha said, "The jug fills drop by drop." Drip it, baby.

92

Don't Give Up Hope
on a Strained Family Relationship

There was a fallout and divide in my family a few years back. Families have more of those than we realize. I always say, if you meet a family that seems "normal," you just don't know them very well.

I didn't speak to one of my sisters for years. Then one day she replied to one of my emails (I still sent her notes now and then, even though we hadn't spoken in a long while). And soon after, she came to New York to visit me. I can say with all sincerity that she's now one of the closest and most loved people in my life.

We talked about the past for only a few minutes, over guacamole and margaritas. Then we came back to the now and forgave everything at once (it really can be that simple).

You get to decide. And while this is true, family isn't always everything. No matter what they tell you. The idea of a stereotypical happy family can be damaging, even. A lot of people have dysfunctional families — and some, no family at all.

The perfect, happy family is more the exception to the rule once you really pay attention. And that's okay.

93

The Pickup Line That Resulted in Two Husbands

*I*t's very sophisticated. Are you ready?
Take notes.
"Hi, I'm Susie."
That's it.
Ha!

Someone has to be bold enough to say hi first. Why not *let it be easy* by letting it be you? It's how you happen to life versus the other way around.

Everyone's scared. But you, my dear, are *willing to be uncomfortable for a moment, aren't you, you confident human being?*

This will result in new, instant relationships, romantic, professional, and friendly. Get out there! Get out, get out, get out! It's where the magic happens!

94

Give People Quantity Time

"*I* have only forty-five minutes — but that's loads of time for a power lunch, right?" I asked my friend Jo, smiling as we sat down at a window table.

"Totally!" she replied as she hugged me.

So we ordered our tomato, basil, and mozzarella sandwiches quickly and dove straight into a shared bag of salt and vinegar chips. We spoke about the usual — work, travel, our husbands, the latest Netflix craze. And forty-five minutes later — on the dot — I grabbed my umbrella and kissed her goodbye on the cheek.

Two weeks later, in a group email to a handful of friends, she told us she was getting divorced and was moving out of her marital home within the month. She didn't need anything; she just wanted us to know.

I was shocked. Why didn't Jo tell me at the café that day? Didn't she feel like she could trust me? I felt a bit confused (and hurt, if I'm honest... I'm a life coach. People normally come to me with this stuff).

Then I realized: *I didn't give her the chance.*

You can't open up about the biggest struggle in your life in forty-five minutes. We always talk about quality time, don't we? But in a go-go-go world, is quality *really* enough? No matter how focused and present we are, doesn't volume have to come into play somewhere? Quality time is powerful and important, but so is *quantity time.*

If you want to build a close relationship with someone — a child, a friend, a new partner, dial up the hours together.

Our deepest, most meaningful relationships in our lives happen over time. In quiet moments. Sometimes in silence or doing nothing special at all, even just watching TV. Just being together is meaningful.

The best investment of your life may come in the form of some real, undivided attention toward someone you care about. Who could use some of yours right now? Could you ask someone you care about? A simple, "Hey — can we spend some time together this week?" will do. And don't settle for a forty-five-minute lunch if you don't have to.

95

Priority Is Meant to Be Singular

The word *priority* is derived from the Latin, meaning "precedence in order or rank," and originally showed up in English in the 1300s. For centuries the word was almost exclusively used in the singular — there was no plural form in its original meaning.

But these days, we have many "priorities" in our busy lives. "Here are my nine business priorities!" my client said once. At that moment, I knew we had some serious work to do. We can pile up priorities to feel busy and important, but in doing so we can lose sight of the most important thing. When you distill things to one priority in each life area — work, health, family — doesn't it feel lighter? It feels better because it's truer. Nine things don't all matter equally. They can't.

We love to make life hard, and having a ton of "priorities" on our mind can give us a false sense of importance. Peel those priorities back. What if you were allowed only one right now? What would it be?

96

The Pursuit of Happiness
Is Miserable

*T*he biggest lie is that life is meant to be perfect and that you're meant to be happy all the time. According to some psych theories, there are only four main emotional states: glad, sad, mad, and scared. And only one of those is positive! We have a whole range of emotions to feel. And the wisdom that will lead us to better-feeling thoughts.

The pursuit of happiness is miserable. It's like searching for an invisible, elusive unicorn — one that's always in the next room, the next job, the next bed.

Esther Hicks says, "A happy life is just a string of happy moments. But most people don't allow the happy moment, because they're so busy trying to get a happy life."

Searching for happiness distracts you from what's already there. And *so much is there*. Look around. The biggest gift you have is your ability to focus. Can you focus on what's going right for thirty seconds?

Even if you just got fired or ghosted (and the date had gone so well!), do you still have the funniest best friend on the planet? Do you still have the comfiest chair in your living room? Does your phone still ring and on the other end is a parent who did their very best for you?

Which four to five things are going right for you right now? List them. And look around. Not everyone is as lucky as you, are they?

97

Drop the Ball Sometimes

*B*ack in my advertising career, a client emailed me once with an urgent question. Normally I'd hop to it and send an answer, pronto. This time I happened to be walking into a barre class, so I gave myself the grace of getting to it when I was finished. By the time I was out, I saw a note from her: "Ignore my last request, I figured it out. Sorry to bother you, Susie!"

Boom. Job done without me.

When I'm overwhelmed, I delay my typical fast responses and see what happens when I don't step in to save the day. Turns out, if you wait just a little, often things work themselves out without you. Exhale!

98

It's Better to Be Happy Than Right

*I*t's not your job to correct everyone on every subject. Or to right every wrong.

I had a consulting client for two years who was, in the beginning, wonderful to me. I sat on the board of the company and secured huge clients for him. Things appeared to be going well. Until his business started losing money. In the end, he owed me $40,000 for hours worked.

After many months of emails back and forth, talk of payment plans, noise, despair, and anger — I had put in so much work and was owed a lot of money, after all — I could have proceeded with a lawsuit, which would have been expensive and likely yielded nothing. So I stopped. In a moment of peace and perfect clarity, I sent this email:

> *You gave me a great consulting opportunity when I transitioned out of my full-time job, which helped me build my now full-time business. I will always appreciate that. Let's*

forget about this debt — I no longer expect it and won't follow up again. Best of wishes to you and your family.

The feeling? Relief. The best human emotion.

Now, don't get me wrong, this isn't me encouraging you to just let people screw you over. And I certainly know that getting to say goodbye to $40,000 is a position not everyone is in, so I'm acknowledging my privilege here. But in that moment, I was grateful to have the option to just say "forget it." It was worth more than $40,000 to let go of the resentment that accompanies a feeling of being effed over. Holding on to resentment like that, I never could have had the focus and clarity that allowed me to create the business I have now.

Can you choose happiness over being right somewhere in your life right now?

Do it for *you*.

99

Anticipatory Fear Is
the Worst Kind of Fear

*D*id you know that looking forward to something — like a vacation or a nice date — is equally (or even more!) enjoyable than the event itself? That's why I don't need surprises. I want to enjoy the event before it even happens.

Turns out that anticipatory fear works the same way.

Happiness researcher Shawn Achor says, "Adversities, no matter what they are, simply don't hit us as hard as we think they will. Our fear of consequences is always worse than the consequences themselves."

I always find this so soothing. *Whatever I'm worrying about right now is worse in my head than it is in real life.* You've survived every bad or hard thing that has happened to you. Right?

You are going to be okay. Ask, *Is my current fear justified? How is it true? How is it not true? How do I feel when the fear is running through my mind? Is it something that I can let go?*

100

Putting Yourself Down Is
Exhausting for Others

I have a friend who is in charge of organizing our group when
it comes to social stuff. She researches and makes dinner res-
ervations, coordinates our time off work, and books our travel
destinations if we all go away together. She loves to be in charge,
and it comes naturally to her.

One time I hit "reply all" to THANK HER AND HER MAD
PLANNING SKILLS in all caps.

She responded, "Oh really? It's nothing."

Other friends piled on more thanks.

She kept rejecting it. So — we stopped. Because it was becoming hard work.

Rejecting a compliment (a gift!) is a drain on the giver. They
are likely not to do it again.

Just say thanks.

101

The Core of Any Phobia
Is a Loss of Control

*H*eights. Flying. Insects that bite. Drunk drivers. Elevators. We hate being out of control, don't we? The best question a life coach or therapist can ask you when you feel like your world is spinning is, "What one thing can you manage in this moment?"

Even when we feel threatened, and the threat is real, there is always, *always* something that we can control. Knowing this grounds us. During the 2020 pandemic, I focused on everything I could control via my actions in my business and the environment that I created at home. I even launched a book at that time, so I took my book tour — all the talks and events — virtual. I made my media pitches as relevant to the time as possible. We are creative beings. Human ingenuity is the most fun part of being human and living among our fellow humans.

What one thing can you manage in this moment? You can sit with this for sixty seconds and just breathe. The answers will come.

Exhale, rise, and get busy.

102

Actions Have Consequences

I was once on *Dr. Oz* giving advice to parents whose kids partake in risky social media challenges (swallowing dice, taking loads of Benadryl to induce hallucinations, the "skull breaker challenge" — the list of dumb stuff that trends can shock you).

Kids, eh? Well — it's not just kids.

My message boiled down was this: *actions have consequences.* And this applies to all of us, young or old. Dramatic decisions and not-so-dramatic decisions. In all life areas. We have an innate ability to think and to reason.

To think and to reason before acting is to walk with wisdom in your life.

Often, we seek immediate pleasure by doing what feels good or fun. I had a friend who bitterly regretted cheating on his girlfriend, who broke it off the second she saw the steamy texts on his phone.

"What was I thinking?" he asked. "I suppose I wasn't thinking much at all."

Hmmm.

Humans are the dominant species on the planet not only because of our superior cognitive ability but also because we have the ability to organize and reason with one another in huge numbers. You can't reason with a dog, although it would be much easier to say, "Hey, it's just the mailman, no need to bark every morning" or to tell a goose, "Why not be adventurous and fly west instead of south this winter? Rumor has it a heat wave is coming to LA!"

But the truth is, while we humans have plenty of advantages, we're also the superior species when it comes to self-sabotage. We can be terrible at reasoning with *ourselves*.

When you remember that every action has a consequence — when you employ your brilliant human brain — might you choose differently? This is what it means to be wise.

103

Ask Yourself, How Much of My Life Was My Idea?

*D*o this when you're craving a change. Really look at your life. How do you spend your money? Where do you live? What do you do on a Saturday night?

How much of it was your idea?

Is it good enough for you? If someone (even you) chose it, and you want to change it, all you have to do is choose again.

Sure, in some area of your life you may very well be a victim of circumstance, but you've also made decisions. A *lot* of them. Are they decisions you want to stick with?

104

Use This Perspective to Relax

*I*f you feel anxious, try putting on a YouTube video about the creation or expansion of the universe, or tune in to a very old movie. Why?

Space reminds you how you're part of something infinite, eternal, mind-boggling. In contrast, what you're worrying about (heck, even your life), is completely insignificant. This should be sobering. Empowering, even.

Our ancestors have been around for six million years. Six million! And humans evolved only two hundred thousand years ago. The Earth was being roamed for 5,800,000 years before we stepped foot on it. We're brand-new! Humbling, right? Of *course* we're just figuring it all out as we go. We're a blip in history. What a way to lose yourself for a while, gain perspective, and take the pressure off.

Old movies evoke a similar emotion. There's something about watching an old classic (where you know all the actors on the screen are now dead) to remind you how temporary everything is.

A hundred years from now, you'll be just like an actress in an old movie. (They'll say, "Wow — people used to wear these things called skinny jeans with rips in them — oh how funny! Shall it be our next party theme, the roaring ripped-jeans 2000s?!") Nothing you have will belong to you anymore — not your body, not your home, and not your prized car, books, or art collection.

It will all be in someone else's hands or in a disposal site somewhere. A new generation will replace us, just as we replaced the last. Enjoy your temporary years! We're here for a loving time, not a long time.

105

Victims Need Villains

*W*hen someone is stuck in a victim loop, they'll find countless villains to blame. The government. The traffic. The weather. Their mother. Someone they cannot control or easily impress or someone who disagrees with them.

We can even *enjoy* seeking the villains, because even if there's drama, something "exciting" is happening and there's still momentum, right?

Is there other, real, useful work you're avoiding? Are you using the drama as a helpful distraction?

Think: Who are the villains in your world? Are there any? Are you giving them a bit too much credit? Are they worthy of such distraction from your purpose and true nature, which is only love?

You're a powerful being who gets to decide how to react to everyone and everything. That's what the victor knows. You have a choice.

106

Never Say, "I Don't Have Time"

Saying, "This isn't a priority" is more truthful.

We all have twenty-four hours in a day. It's up to us to decide how we spend those hours. To say you don't have time for something really means you don't want to do it.

You can replace it with these statements instead:

"That's not a priority for me right now."

"I can take that project on, but I will need [x amount of time] to complete it."

"Right now, my focus is on x; perhaps [another person] is better placed to help?"

Saying "I don't have time" is a bit of a lie, really — when we all have it in equal measure. It's akin to when we hear people say, "I can't afford that." People say it all the time, when what they really mean is, "I'm not interested in that." That's okay, but let's say what we mean!

We can be more honest and assertive about how we're spending our time (and for that matter, moola).

107

Humans Are Wired for Mimicry

*W*hat happens when you see someone yawn? Or sit among a group of people laughing uncontrollably? You yawn and laugh, too, right? That's because of our in-built mirror neurons.

Mirror neurons fire both when we act and when we observe the same action being performed by another person. Thus, the neuron "mirrors" the behavior of the other, as though the observer were itself acting. We match what is before us!

Use this to your advantage. When I was an au pair and a kid fell and scraped her hands, I'd laugh and say, "Get back up, scooter princess!" The kid would look confused for a second, smile slowly, and then get back up and zoom off again.

If you feel bad that you can attend only half a meeting or event, instead of showing up apologetic and meek, be enthusiastic. Say, "I'm thrilled I could be here for part of this!"

Our mirror neurons mean the world will always respond to us in kind. Show up the way you want to be mirrored.

108

Take It Seriously, but Hold It Lightly

A friend of mine commented once that my work looks like a lot of fun, that she would love to be like me and go through life "taking nothing too seriously." I found this interesting.

It's true that I do have fun working. I sing on Zoom calls. I go to lunch spontaneously and laugh a lot. People think that being fun and light and being serious are mutually exclusive. I consciously make my day fun and exciting. Why wouldn't I? Why wouldn't you? Your life is in session — add music!

Where can you add energizing fun filters to your day? Success orbits around joy — not the other way around. Joy removes stress and makes us more creative. Wearing it all lightly and with fun makes life more enjoyable and makes me better at my job. I see people whose work is similar to my own but who focus on the stresses, pressure, and uncertainty of it all. I feel sad that they miss the joy of why we're all here in the first place.

"Nice work if you can get it, Susie."

Yep — it is nice. And you can get it!

You can be serious *and* light.

109

Be Generous in Order to Win

*M*y first job ever was in a bakery in England. I was fifteen, and I lived for the free iced buns (I'd turn away from the security camera, take secret bites, and feel like Angelina Jolie getting away with a sexy screen crime).

The bakery had a takeout lunch special one weekend that they were testing. It was a sandwich and a cup of tea for just £4 (oh, the early 2000s — don't get me all wistful now). The chef in the back would skimp on the tuna in the sandwich.

"Rick, what do you call this?" I'd ask, holding two flimsy slices of bread stuck together with what seemed like just mayonnaise.

"They don't get more tuna than that for four quid!"

"Rick, this special won't last very long with this sad, little *I-need-a-microscope-to-see-the-tuna* sandwich."

When we hold back, we may think we're being responsible or practical or self-respecting. But life doesn't work that way. Generosity begets generosity. Give people more than they expect. I can't tell you how many times people tell me I need to raise my prices, but I know who I am and what I want — as many people in my world as possible. Not just the few who can afford a higher price tag.

Scoop up the tuna, and serve generously! Then see the line out the door.

110

Give the People You Love
Permission to Die

*W*e often think that strength is all about holding on, but sometimes it's about letting go. My mum, whose work in Africa included working with people with HIV/AIDS, taught me the importance of giving people "permission" to die.

My mum would help people grieve over the loss of a loved one. Sometimes they would refuse to acknowledge that an impending death was inevitable. They'd fight it, saying to the person who was dying, "Hey, you're getting better — you'll be fine soon!"

Mum would tell them that there is strength and courage in letting go. That we put pressure on people to live because we fear our own suffering and loss instead of focusing on their release from pain.

To die and to be missed is to be alive because love is stronger than death. We fear death, but death is just proof that we lived. And the sadness that comes with it means that you loved. Life is like summer flowers; death like autumn leaves. There's beauty in all things.

111

Desire Requires
Distance Sometimes

*H*eath and I aren't just married; we also work together. So we spend a *lot* of time together. Most couples bicker about nothing juicy in particular, but occasionally Heath and I end up just not giving each other enough space. One time, I was about to embark on a girls' trip, and I was excited to get away for a bit and have some peace and distance. But when I got to my room and saw the water view and heard laughter from a couple by the pool, I missed him. And how he pretends to be a shark in swimming pools and grabs my legs as I attempt to jump out (I pretend to hate it but I secretly love his playfulness).

It instantly reminded me of a line from Kahlil Gibran's book *The Prophet* that I read at a friend's wedding: "Let there be spaces in your togetherness ..."

I thought about it as I spoke to my friends that evening. I asked them when they feel most in love with their partners. Here's some of what I heard:

"When I see him playing competitive tennis, that's hot!"

"When I read his end-of-year reviews from his team and they rave about his compassionate leadership."

"When he comes back from a conference where he spoke onstage and I see the pics and comments, I'm just reminded of what I felt so attracted to in the first place."

Desire doesn't require get-on-a-plane distance. It means having space at home, on the weekends, having hobbies for yourself. Gibran says, "The oak tree and the cypress grow not in each other's shadow."

Resparking your desire isn't just about staring into each other's eyes over candlelight. It's also about remembering that you are two individuals and about appreciating the parts of each other's lives that don't have to do with you. Allow yourself to miss and be missed, even in small ways.

112

Unused Talents May as Well Not Exist

*A*esop was a legendary Greek fabulist (meaning a writer of fables — isn't that a wonderful word?). Here are a few of his most famous:

The story of the hare and the tortoise; slow and steady wins the race.

The warning about the boy who cried wolf; a liar will not be believed even when he tells the truth.

The fox and his sour grapes; it's easy to despise what you cannot get.

Aesop was a slave who lived in the sixth century BCE and eventually was freed by his master because of his wisdom and wit. It was said that he earned his freedom through his storytelling and went on to serve as adviser to a king. Not too bad a transformation, eh? That's the power of wisdom.

This is my favorite fable of his. It's called "The Miser and His Gold":

Once upon a time there was a miser who used to hide his gold at the foot of a small tree in his garden, but every week he used to go and dig it up and gloat over his gains. A robber, who had noticed this, went and dug up the gold and stole it. When the miser next came to gloat over his treasures, he found nothing but the empty hole. He tore his hair and raised such an outcry that all the neighbors came around him, and he told them how he used to come and visit his gold.

"Did you ever take any of it out?" asked one of them.

"Nay," said he, "I only came to look at it."

"Then come again and look at the hole," said a neighbor. "It will do you just as much good."

The moral of the story: *wealth unused might as well not exist.*

Inside each and every one of us is gold. It can feel hard to use it, I know. Life gets in the way. Work. Kids. To-do lists. Never-ending emails. Social media distractions. Hundreds of things pulling us in different directions. Distractions come at you from all sides, right?

Getting the important stuff done matters. Otherwise, our lives are frittered away on meetings, happy hours, TV reruns, and Instagram. You need to schedule time to achieve your goals. It's a nonnegotiable, ongoing appointment you keep with yourself.

Because nothing beats action. A book won't write itself. Your body won't magically manifest itself in a spin studio. Your dating life won't double overnight as you sit on the sofa, eating Oreos. You gotta get busy!

How can you make time for the important and not just the urgent day-to-day? Your gold matters because your life matters. Don't leave it in the hole at the bottom of your get-to-do list, okay?

113

Happiness Is a Short Memory

*M*y father-in-law is an avid golfer. From my limited knowledge of the sport, I know there are good rounds and bad rounds. And that you can play for years and still play terribly at unexpected moments. "The happiest golfers have a short memory, Susie!" he said to me once, after a bad day on the course.

There's a life lesson here, I thought. I'm happiest when I forget about:

- mean reviews
- the snarky woman at Dunkin' Donuts
- the cancel fee on a workout class I didn't attend because I was tired
- a passive-aggressive comment from a relative
- the newish lip balm I left in an Uber

Can you have a selectively short memory, too? What would you *lose* if you forgot that your partner didn't notice your haircut? Or that your friend forgot your birthday? (Hey, I only remember birthdays because of Facebook — thanks, Zuckers!) What do you *gain* by hanging on to these memories?

You'll see how having a short memory gets you back out there faster.

114

When in Doubt, Zoom Out

*O*ften a client will say to me, "I screwed up." They say it like it's the end of the world. And I get it — it can feel that way when we're in the moment and mad at ourselves. They didn't take the action or do the uncomfortable thing that would have propelled them forward (an Instagram Live, a request for collaboration with someone, a hard conversation — *scary is good*, as we know). They "cheated" during a booze or sugar break. They didn't launch the business.

My friend Adam put the highs and lows of life so succinctly one day when I told him I felt behind on a long-term project. We were having lunch at a sushi restaurant in Miami. He took a bite of crispy rice and said, "Susie, look, anything worth doing takes time. It's like the stock market. If you check it every day, you'll freak out. If you take an aerial view, zoom out, and see the progress over time, you'll see the line goes upward."

Progress can feel deceitful if you check in and take score too often and too soon. What happens if you zoom out for a sec? How does the you of today compare to the you of a year ago? Go easier on yourself. You're doing a better job than you think. Wisdom is patient.

When in doubt, zoom out.

115

Deflate Drama with Distraction

*W*hen I was eighteen years old, I was an au pair in the Languedoc region in the South of France. The eldest child under my care, six-year-old Alizee, taught me a lesson I'll never forget.

When there was a new toy to play with (or an old toy plucked out of a stack of games that felt new and exciting again) Alizee and her four-year-old sister would have a party with it — until their toddler brother saw it and screamed until he could hold it. Alizee would swiftly pick up one of his toys and marvel at it, and her little bro would stretch out his little chubby arms toward his own bright gadget. Everyone was happy.

If I feel a conversation getting heated (that I sense won't be a helpful debate or a helpful sharing of information), I'll talk about the food, an upcoming event, or frankly anything else. I'll pick a new toy to deflate the drama.

Adults aren't tantrummy toddlers, but all humans can benefit from the right distraction at the right time.

116

Say Sorry First

*R*emember that scene in *Home Alone* when the next-door neighbor makes up with the son he hasn't spoken to in years (he has to go to church to see his niece sing in the choir because he's not welcome at their house)? And when you see them reunite, you...well...*cue waterworks.*

Sweet little Kevin encourages the older man to call his son. We all agree when he encourages this, with his childlike innocence, and we're thrilled when we see the family together. As I've said before, family isn't necessarily everything. And not every relationship is healthy and worthy of repair.

But when it is important to you, do you have the courage to say sorry first? To be the one who reaches out to make amends? Admit that you made a mistake? Even if you feel like you didn't make the biggest one or that you're owed an apology, too? We *all* make mistakes, after all — and to be honest, we all make them all the time! Peaceful people understand that our position in an argument is not more important than our happiness.

Saying sorry requires strength and humility, and *it's not immediately easy*. But do you value the person who wants your apology? Even if they're wrong, have you been wrong, too? Think about it for twenty seconds without defense. Humility and love are often matched once someone has the willingness to go first. You'll notice that when you have the courage and humility to say sorry, often people become less defensive in an instant and more loving toward you. But someone has to go first. On your deathbed, will it matter who "should" have apologized first? Small resentments can turn into years of silence. They don't have to.

Sorry is a strong person's word. (CrossFit not required.)

117

Build Trust with Yourself

*W*hen I was six years old, I lived in a domestic-abuse shelter with my mum and sister. Pretty soon, I sorted the other kids I met in the shelter into two groups: the temporary shelter friends and the more permanent kind.

Some women would arrive with their families, stay for a few nights, and then move on. They'd had their "walk-out" moment and decided they'd had enough. They needed help for a while, then got organized and set up new homes and lives for their families. The other group would come and go a lot. My mum explained that women with low self-esteem often go back to their abusers — and get the same treatment — and then come back to the shelter. They were completely swayed by a phone call, a promise, or the 317,480,534th apology they'd been offered.

One woman, Maria, was kinda in between. I observed her with curiosity. Like my mum, she had five kids. Maria was a lot of fun — she snuck me a spoonful of the fancy ice cream reserved just for the grown-ups once, and this was even *after* I'd brushed my teeth. She often dangled her youngest kids by their ankles for fun, making everyone laugh.

Maria did go back to her abusive ex, but she did it just the one time. After she returned to the shelter for the second time, she was done. She said to my mum, "Nina, no more. I mean it this time."

And that was it. She moved away to be closer to her relatives and sent my mum a letter saying, "I trust myself now. Everything is different."

Where did that trust come from? Following through on her intention to put herself first. I've always remembered it.

This illustrates something important: trust in yourself comes from follow-through. The same way that you ditch a flaky friend who always cancels on your morning walk or seek out a new job when you realize your boss doesn't have your back, you take responsibility for what's happening in your life — big and small.

Are you following through for yourself? If you do it for just a day to start with (do the workout, write a blog post, return the shoes that don't fit, eat what you have in the fridge versus last-minute ordering in again), you'll begin building trust with yourself.

Trust is earned through actions, big and small. You're worthy of them all.

118

People Who Don't Trust
Can't Be Trusted

*A*n old acquaintance of mine called me gullible because I
believe what I'm told. We were together at an event, and I
was sending a DM to a successful author to congratulate her on a
career win she posted about. I happily mentioned it to my acquaintance, and she said, "You believe her? I want receipts!"

I felt like a fool for a bit after she said that. I thought, *Have
I been believing lies my whole life? Is the world this big lie-packed,
dangerous, everyone-is-out-to-get-you kinda place?*

Then I thought about it.

The acquaintance who was so distrustful might not be a trustworthy woman herself. Like the jealous boyfriend who suspects
you of cheating because *he's the one* cheating. She didn't have
many long-term friends (we only met once or twice; I instinctively didn't feel inclined after that). And she had only negative
stories about other people. Lao Tzu said, "He who does not trust
enough, will not be trusted."

Pay attention when someone cannot trust or believe in other people. There is a valuable lesson here — because modest doubt is wise. They might not be worthy of *your* trust. Because we see what we are. Our external world matches our internal world.

Hey, I'd rather be gullible *and* trustworthy.

119

Know Your One Thing

*W*hat one thing can you do to make your life easier? This is a fun question to ask. When I've asked groups of people, here are some of the answers I've gotten:

- Get up at the same time every day
- Quit drinking
- Marie Kondo my apartment
- Hire some help
- Stop nitpicking in my relationship
- Forgive someone
- Start a side hustle (for career options as well as money)
- Find a good coach
- Create a daily structure
- Set aside 20 minutes to read at night before bed
- Delete food delivery apps
- Start a podcast
- Sell myself more!

Remember, success isn't passive. We don't have to turn our lives upside down to get rid of the hard and find ease. Ease can be driven by a simple thing. All areas of our lives are connected and spill into the other areas. What might your one thing be? Just think about it.

120

See the Child in Everyone

*I*f you ever feel like you need help forgiving (or even just liking) someone, try this. Picture them as a kid. Imagine how they looked. Their little face, their little hands and feet. Shy, curious, not knowing any better. See the innocent humanness in them.

This is who you are still dealing with now — just taller and older. And probably hardened and disappointed by life to some degree.

Do you need to do this with your parents, perhaps?

My mum was the last person to see my dad alive. Near the end of his life he was alone and scared, and he called her and asked her to come to him. She got straight on the train (without even brushing her hair) to be with him. She said that in that moment, she forgot the years of physical and emotional abuse. She thought about one thing — the five-year-old sensitive Peter who was shipped to boarding school and ran away to see his mum, "just for a minute!" before the police sent him back without obliging him. My mum kissed my dad's forehead for the last time and later told me, "Susie, I didn't kiss a dying man — I kissed a five-year-old boy who wanted his mum."

Can you see your mum and dad as young children, age four or five? As in, really see them? Imagine them as vividly as you can. They didn't have perfect parents either. What was their childhood like? What scared them? *What happened to them?*

Even better is doing this for yourself. Keep a photo of you as a kid close by (I keep mine as a phone screensaver sometimes — because I love her). I think, *Would I talk to "little Susie" the way I'd talk to adult me?* No.

I'm kinder. More relaxed and forgiving with her. When she makes mistakes I say, "It's okay, get back up, little one — let's go!" And we do.

121

Love Is What Makes a Family

hen my mum and I were living in a women's shelter, we'd
watch a popular old English TV show, *Blind Date*, on the
small black-and-white TV. It was the highlight of our Saturday
night for years.

On the show, a girl and a guy each get to choose one out of
three suitors based on the suitors' answers to their question —
without seeing them. When they choose, there's the big reveal
when the divider is pulled back and they see each other for the
first time, embrace, and then go away for a weekend together.

To a kid, this show was thrilling, and watching it with my
mum made it even better, as she would always pepper in her
commentary: "She should choose him, he has kind eyes" or "He
should choose her, she's sincere and educated."

One night, after a particularly fun show, I was holding my
mum's hand, walking up the stairs to our shared room.

"We have the best family!" I told her.

My mum said that as an anxiety-filled single mum on welfare, without a home or a sense of security, she felt such relief and joy at hearing this. I don't actually remember saying this to her (I was only six!), but she told me about it years later and what it had meant to her then.

Around that time, my sister and I went to a summer camp that was held by the Salvation Army for kids like me. As the youngest of five girls, I was delighted to meet a sweet new friend, Ebony, who was a year younger than me. The whole time, we pretended to be sisters. I loved being a "big sister" for a week and showing sweet Ebony how to tuck the bottom of her T-shirt into the collar so that she had a crop top. And revealing to her a couple of the "bad words" that grown-ups use "that you should never say" because I was older and in the know. And obviously cool.

On the last day, as we packed our little red rucksacks and hugged goodbye, Ebony said to me, "I wish you were my real sister."

I often think of Ebony. And I hope life is kind to her wherever she is.

Two parents don't make a family. Neither does blood, kids, a golden retriever, or anything else you see in the movies.

I've now lived in five countries without family close by, but I have strong, loyal, and close friendships, and I know this to be true: families come in all shapes and sizes.

Because all that makes a family is love.

122

Four Words to Be Wary of Using

*T*hese are innocent words. But I feel a little *ding* inside when I hear other people, and myself, use them. They're not swear words. Or even critical words — which is why they're a bit insidious.

Here they are:

Always. Never. Everybody. Nobody.

Be conscious of using these words!

I know I'm on thin ice in a fight with Heath when I say, "You're always on your phone when I'm talking...," or he says, "You never help me tidy up ..."

Very rarely, if ever, are *always* and *never* true. They are not helpful.

Same with *everybody* and *nobody*.

"Nobody likes me / would read my book / cares about my social media posts!"

"Everybody already has a life coach / personal organizer / YouTube channel they go to for this stuff."

Really? Notice how we typically use these all-or-nothing words against ourselves when we're trying to discourage ourselves from something we want or when we're picking a fight with someone?

Words have power. Sticking to the truth is much easier (and much more helpful).

123

When You Want to Give Up, Remember This

I love the story about a tribe in Africa that is always called on when there is a drought because, somehow, they can always make it rain with their dancing rituals. It confused anthropologists. How can dancing create rain? Surely not. But they were reported to have a 100 percent success rate.

They did nothing that the other tribes in the region didn't do: they offered the same prayers, the same incantations, the same moves. All the rituals were very similar to those of the tribes around them. And like all the other tribes, they would dance for days or weeks. But this tribe opened the skies and the rain came down.

A member of the tribe was interviewed and asked the question, "How do you always make it rain? It seems impossible!"

He answered something that I repeat to myself whenever I want to give up.

"Oh, we dance *until it rains.*"

Persistence wins. It's not glamorous or magical, which is good news. Anyone can do it, if they're willing.

124

Live and Let Live —
the Ultimate Wisdom

*T*he first three first words of this book's title are "Let It Be." They're also the name of a famous Beatles song.

Letting it be is easier than it looks sometimes. I was once at a dinner party with a friend who is a prominent financial journalist. James knows all about interest rates, investments, retirement planning, and everybody's favorite new dinner party conversation: cryptocurrencies. A few glasses of wine in, another guy at the table had a strong point of view on Bitcoin that James knew to be categorically false. I could tell by how he straightened his back and widened his eyes as he listened.

Oh no, I thought. *This poor guy.* James is going to destroy him. I tried to change the subject to avoid the inevitable debate that would follow, but Mr. Crypto wouldn't hear of it. He was spewing "all the facts."

James surprised me. He said *not a single word.* He sipped his sparkling water and tucked into his cheesecake. He let it be.

"James!" I exclaimed as we walked toward the elevator at the end of the evening. "Why didn't you correct that guy? You have the actual facts!"

"Susie, I came for a fun evening with you. It's not my job to correct other people. I can let them be wrong and enjoy my evening with you."

I was impressed. He was right. *Hey — did anyone ever say that it's better to be happy than right?* I felt an unexpected relief in that moment. Maybe I could do more of that, too. Letting it be. Perhaps the best way to win an argument is to avoid it altogether.

Ever notice how the happiest people are the least judgmental? They don't throw shade at how other people live or think. They just focus quietly on themselves and allow others the same space. It's another version of the Golden Rule: do unto others as you would have them do unto you.

Do you want to be judged or proved wrong? Is that helpful? Do you change for the better when someone is judgmental toward you? You can live your life without having others validate it for you. You can also live your life without needing to invalidate someone else's. Can you just let others be? Not everything needs exploration and understanding. There simply isn't time for this if we want to fulfill our destiny.

What's it to you how other people choose to live? Does it concern you? Do you need to correct others? If so — enjoy the headache. One of my biggest freedoms now is letting people be wrong about *me*, even. I don't set strangers on the internet straight, and it might be one of my most underrated acts of self-care.

You're not the general manager of the universe. You're responsible just for the corner of the world that you touch. Give your mind a rest, and enjoy the cheesecake.

125

Nostalgia Is Dangerous

*D*o you ever feel like your life is missing something? Do you sometimes look back at a happier time when everything was better? I had drinks with an old coworker in New York once, and he told me he didn't like his new job too much — it had a steep and demanding learning curve. He said, "Remember those cool conferences we'd have as a team in San Francisco? Man, those were the good old days!"

I smiled. Yes, they were.

But in my quest to be a little objective, I remembered it a little differently. We had plenty of fun back then, certainly. But I also remembered, if I recall the full picture, being stressed-out and tired from so much work travel, being irritated by the company's goals always changing, and a little unhappy with a micromanaging boss.

You might be right: there was a happy time in your past. But it might not be exactly how you remember it in your haste to discount and skip over the present.

The you that you see in pictures now, you'll marvel at in ten years.

The stuff you're learning right now might give you pangs of nostalgia in the future (notice how every entrepreneur loves to share the kitchen desk or garage photo of when they started out)?

The pain you might be feeling now could be the start of a beautiful detour in a new direction. The good old days are happening now, too. We don't want to miss them, do we? Perhaps it's time to allow the present, no matter how imperfect it may seem, to be good anyway.

Can you allow yourself to enjoy "the good old days" while you're still in them?

126

Too Late Is a Decision, Not a Position

*T*here's nothing worse than adding milk to your tea, taking a sip, and discovering that the milk is…sour. Eep. You check the carton and the expiration date tells you it went off days ago. The milk has a "line-in-the-sand" expiration. Do not use it after this date — it will taste gross and might make you sick.

But why on earth would we think humans have an expiration date? Let's say we did. When would it be? Age thirty-five? Forty? Fifty-seven? *Says who?* And for what practical reason? As Oprah says, "So long as there is breath in your body, there is more."

I love to hear stories of people who started things at later life stages. My mum went back to school in her midfifties to study childhood education. Julia Child released her first cookbook at fifty. Vera Wang entered the fashion industry at forty. Harriet Doerr published her first novel at seventy-four.

You are not behind. When people come to me hoping to launch a new venture but think they might be "too late," they overlook the fact that they already know so much. Their experience is a huge advantage, not something to underplay or discount. No experience is wasted. It can be gloriously transferred. I work with former ("recovering" they tell me) lawyers who now coach stepmoms to navigate the challenges of a blended family. Accountants who create art and sell it all over the world. Didn't they get the memo that January 1, 2013, was their expiration date and that they're breaking the rules? I guess not. Someone should arrest them.

I once heard an investor say, "We prefer to invest in slightly older CEOs. They've experienced more. They can be wiser. We have better outcomes with them."

It's never too late.

127

Raise Your Hand Even When You Don't Know the Answer

*I*n our unwillingness to be uncomfortable, we give up a lot. It's hard even to know how much is available unless we try.

Don't want to ask someone out?

Get a new client?

Put your hat in the ring for an opportunity?

It's true that you may not get the result you want if you try. But success is volume!

I love what author Seth Godin says: *"You need to press the buzzer before you know the answer."* In a game show setting like *Jeopardy*, you should buzz as soon as you realize that you will probably be able to identify the answer by the time you're asked. Between the time you buzz and the time you're supposed to speak, the answer will come to you. And if it doesn't, the penalty for being wrong is small compared to the missed opportunity to get it right.

The same is true in life.

No author is certain their book will sell.

No one going on a blind date knows where the relationship will go.
No entrepreneur knows if they're making the *correct* business moves.

You either just buzz or you don't. You try and *may* lose, or you don't try and *definitely* lose. You can't win if you pause too long and never hit the buzzer. Life is about taking risks. If you don't risk, you don't live. Can you trust that the answer will come, just by giving it a chance? It's not recklessness, it's courage. It's being in the arena, not the audience.

A boss said to me once, "Go for the big clients, Susie! Some will reject you for sure. Some won't. You'll get rejection no matter what, so you might as well get paid."

Buzz away.

128

There's Nothing Uncool
about Practice

"*I* practiced his name a few times so I could say it to his face,"
a friend once told me, referring to the guy he had a crush on
at the gym.

"Ethan! Hi, Ethan. Yo, Ethan!" he'd say in the mirror, practic-
ing a casual smile.

I thought it was just the coolest, most honest thing to share.
I mean, haven't we all been there? And when he finally spoke to
Ethan at the break bench one early morning, their conversation
was easy.

In a world that celebrates shortcuts and quick wins and overnight success, we forget that practice is essential to gain. This
is true for any worthwhile skill, from introducing yourself to a
stranger to mastering a sport or language.

People don't talk about practice much, do they? We just see
the end result of perseverance. And we are so hard on ourselves
because other people can do all these impressive things, and we
can't. And we think life is so much easier for other people, who

can "suddenly" ice-skate, write articles, get by in a country with a foreign language, or whip up a tasty meal in ten minutes.

We don't see what goes on behind the scenes. The early mornings in the rink. The edits and rewrites of an article. The embarrassment of saying something in Spanish to a confused-looking Spaniard. The four to five nights a week someone cooks for themselves instead of ordering takeout. The frustration at failing again and again. The alarm clock that goes off at 6:00 a.m.

My favorite definition of happiness is "the joy we experience as we move toward our potential."

It's easy to watch TV reruns and sleep in (and we should when we need to)! Just don't fool yourself that other people are talented and you're not. They practice. They stay in the game. They shake off the unwanted results and keep at it.

I beg you to find an exception and share it with me. I have never found one.

What we practice, we become. Can you be easy about some things taking time? They take time because they're worth it. If a little dedication weren't required, we'd all be walking around with six-pack abs and a billion dollars.

129

Find Commonalities
with Your "Enemies"

*O*ne time, when I was working in Washington, DC, in my corporate job, I met the wife of a client at a steakhouse bar where a few of us were gathered. From what I understood, she and her husband had a pretty traditional marriage with conventional gender roles. And when she joined us that evening, she said to me over crab cakes and chardonnay, "Doesn't your husband mind your traveling for work alone? Steve would not like that for a second!"

I could tell that she and I were different and probably valued different things. And that this could be a divisive and uncomfortable conversation if we let it be. As an ambitious professional without kids, I felt like this woman and I wouldn't have much in common. And I thought for a second, *Oh my, we're going to have nothing to talk about — this could be awkward.*

"Nah," I answered, "my husband loves to play Nintendo in peace, and I live for the spa at the W Hotel — it works for us!"

My new friend and I immediately bonded over the spa's silky

skin-care products. Then she told me that she went away with her sister for her fortieth birthday and that Steve appreciated her like crazy the second she stepped through the door. (Yep — did anyone say "desire requires distance sometimes"?)

We spoke about marriage, travel, and how to cook a gourmet, restaurant-quality steak at home (it's all about frying up a piece of bacon in the pan first, a cooking gem that I've since used)!

Not only did we have a good time, I was learning things. This would not have happened if I thought, *We have nothing in common, I need to switch seats with someone!*

Sometimes we'll disagree fervently with another person. And sometimes we give that point of disagreement a magnifying glass — at the cost of understanding what we have in common with the other person.

To paraphrase author Mike Dooley: Friends are friends because they've discovered how much they have in common. Enemies are people who have not yet discovered this.

This woman was not *my enemy*. But often we write people off before giving them a chance when we just know a bit of information about them that clashes with our own beliefs or lifestyles. You might have the same sense of humor, a similar parenting style, a love of the same books and TV shows, and the same passion for the arts as someone else, but you may discount all that if someone has a different view on family, religion, or politics than you do.

And then, that's it! The object of disagreement gets all the airtime. Can you ... let it be? You might even be aligned in 90 percent of other things. And that's a lot!

Maybe we can even learn something from someone we

disagree with, as I did (and I now know how to make a juicy rib-eye on my stove, thank you very much). This requires putting the ego aside for a minute. It requires seeking commonalities instead of differences. Every other person can in some way be our teacher. And a trigger you feel (that negative charge in your body) might give you something new and even expansive to think about.

This is why I love to read articles with completely different points of view than my own. I want to keep an open mind about the world.

Choosing love goes a long way. Can you disagree on something and let it be okay? Don't brush off the 90 percent that still stands.

130

Let Selling Be Easy

*O*ne of my favorite things to do in my business is help people sell more. Sales can seem scary, but it's simple, really — it's just a value exchange. You give something of value, and someone gives you material currency for it. That's it. We create a lot of stories in our minds about it though, don't we?

Life is selling, day after day, whether you're trying to convince your partner to go out for dinner, your kid (or adult partner, ahem!) to turn off the Xbox, or your boss to give you a raise. We're all selling, all the time, even though we don't call it that.

So how do we make selling easier? By understanding a little better how persuasion works. Nothing illustrates the magic and simplicity of persuasion more beautifully than Aesop's fable "The North Wind and the Sun":

The wind and the sun have a dispute over which is stronger. The wind spots a traveler and tells the sun, "Watch me make him take off his coat!" But the stronger he blows, the tighter the traveler pulls his coat to this body. Then the sun takes her turn. She beams warm and loving rays at the traveler until he willingly undresses.

The moral? Persuasion is far more effective than force. Always has been, always will be. How can you be more persuasive — at home, at work, in your relationships?

By using the Four Ps framework!

Purpose

What do you want to achieve in persuading someone? Have a clear objective. Can you measure whether or not you were effective? For example, do you want a 20 percent salary increase? Do you want a date night every Friday? Do you want your kid to limit video games to forty-five minutes a day? Having a clear purpose in mind makes you confident because clarity does not allow for confusion or mixed messages. What's your precise purpose when it comes to your next persuasion?

Prepare

This step is commonly overlooked as we dive straight into making requests. What's the *why* behind your purpose? Why does it matter?

For example, if you want a raise, how much money are people in your role being paid at different companies? How have you gone above and beyond in your position over the past twelve months? Make a list of that good stuff. How has your company benefited as a direct result of your contribution? Preparation puts you in the strongest stance possible. Added bonus: Prepare for the rebuttals you might get. Play devil's advocate with yourself. Prepare a comeback for every possible rejection!

Present (with Presence)

When we want someone to do something, we want to present the decision or option in their best interest. For instance, I was negotiating a conference room in a nice hotel and wanted to pay way less than the standard fee. I didn't mention my limited budget. I didn't talk about my needs. I didn't appeal in an apologetic way.

What I did do was tell the events manager that twenty of New York's finest entrepreneurs would come to her hotel, see its amazing facilities, be introduced to the chain, potentially book rooms, and even consider hosting their own conferences there (meaning: more money is gonna be coming your way, girlfriend)! Your language and the vision you create matters. My objective was to get a 40 percent discount. I got a 30 percent. Win-win for all!

It's important to be as present as you can be when presenting your case. Everyone just wants to be heard, so be an active listener and present with presence!

Persevere — and Be Patient!

Someone once said that 80 percent of success is showing up. *I'd argue it's staying put once you get there.* We are too likely to quit, walk away, and leave dissatisfied from any negotiation. After almost two decades in sales, I can tell you that the best salespeople simply stay in the arena. It's true that success is a numbers (and patience) game — and most people just leave the party too early.

Say your company doesn't have the budget for salary increases until the spring. Cool! Follow up in April. What can they give you in the interim — maybe some additional time off? A more flexible work-from-home option? It's okay to keep asking questions. Remember all the prep you did — you're an awesome team player and have plenty of reasons you deserve it — but if you don't ask, the answer is always going to be no, and giving up will get you nowhere.

Force can give you a short win, yes, but the long game is all about providing value and making that value clear. Let your prospect slip off their coat.

Easier, right?

131

Be Flexible When
Unexpected Things Happen

I love a plan. I can picture it. Feel it. Expect it. Make moves
and predictions. It feels exciting and real! But sometimes life
happens and plans get thrown off. Someone lets you down. The
weather changes. A verbal agreement never comes to fruition on
paper. A house sale falls through. Someone gets sick and has to
cancel.

This stresses people out. And that's natural! But what I've
found is that when we're flexible, a remarkable thing happens. We
relax — and everyone else around us relaxes, too. Creative solu-
tions abound. Stress shuts off the brain, quite literally. It compro-
mises the function of higher executive areas in the human brain
that allow idea flow. When we're afraid, we revert to our most
fear-based, most primitive state.

When you can ease into flexibility, it's surprising how produc-
tive you can become. Instead of focusing on what's wrong, you
can focus on what's possible under new circumstances. Focus is

the key. The same way that, when you're driving, the car will go where your eyes go, outcomes will follow the point of your focus.

A friend of mine told me about an outdoor wedding she went to that went awry when "partly cloudy" moved to rain sprinkles to full-on sun showers. Because the bride was prepared and flexible, she had cute umbrellas at the ready. She smiled as she dabbed her forehead and cheek as her husband said his vows. Her ease put everyone else at ease.

I wanted to meet her; I already liked her.

One Day, You Won't Even Be a File in a Hospital

I read once that if you die in a hospital and there will be no assumed future use for your medical record, your file is shredded. A few years after you die, *there will be no record of your ever having been there.*

Learning this filled me with unexpected relief and made me feel like it's even more important to put myself out there while I still have time. Just think: one day, you won't even be a file in a hospital.

So live now! Do things now! Don't take it all so seriously! There won't even be a record! Feel that itch to get busy and create more?

Do we have to be so scared when we create? A new generation is coming in no time. Can you show up for yours? It's all temporary, so enjoy it! Nothing else feels quite as regret-proof.

Replace Your Knife with an Ax

*A*braham Lincoln said, "If I only had an hour to chop down a tree, I would spend the first forty-five minutes sharpening my ax."

This is how I feel about learning new skills — it's like replacing a kitchen knife with an ax. Learning a new skill takes some time, but it saves time later. Ultimately, isn't *not* learning something harder than actually just learning it? And besides, learning keeps us young!

When I started my business, I had to learn about email marketing, advertising, and a few new technical platforms. It all felt like a headache at first. Until it didn't. We never stop upgrading our skills. It can feel hard before we learn more, and then, just as with any new skill, it becomes easy.

But when you have a few axes in the mix, you're a magnet for ease.

What one skill can you learn that will make your life easier?

Batch Your Life!

I love the term *batch*.

It makes me think of a batch of cookies or muffins, fresh from the oven, making the whole house smell like Martha Stewart just floated out the front door.

And that's a helpful way to think about it. We don't create one cookie or muffin at a time, we create a dozen or so. Life is like this, too. We typically don't just send one email a day, or have one meeting on a Monday, or clean one plate — then watch TV — then clean another — then nap — then clean the rest.

But often when we're trying to focus on something, we act like we're baking one muffin at a time.

When we switch things up too frequently, moving from email to social media to washing dishes back to email, we carry what's called "attention residue" to each task as we switch. Our attention is split when we have multiple tasks active at once, diminishing our overall performance.

So can you batch what you're doing? Check and reply to emails at two set times of day? Write your book first thing in the morning with your phone in a drawer? Just clean the whole bloody kitchen while you have those rubber gloves on and the music is crankin'?

You'll be surprised at how swiftly things can be completed. It's like combining a marathon *and* a sprint (a... mint?). Yes, you'll do things in quick bursts. But even marathon runners don't stop to check email, do some online shopping, or call their grandmas mid-race.

Do similar things at once, in a batch — for speed and to keep your sanity!

The Best Way to Make a Friend

A client of mine told me she finds it hard to make "real friends." After discussing what she does to meet new people — it turned out she does quite a bit — I asked her, "How much of a friend are you being to the people you meet?" She was confused.

"They don't text me to go out! They didn't check in when I said I wasn't feeling well. They don't, they don't ..."

I asked, "Do you text them and ask them to meet? Do you check in on them to see how they're doing?"

She admitted she didn't. It's funny how much we expect from others when we're not actively showing up the way we want others to. Eckhart Tolle said, "What you think is being withheld from you, you are withholding from the world."

In other words, what we want to get, we need to give first. A beautiful concept, really. The best way to make a friend is to be one. A simple concept, but easily overlooked. Are you the kind of friend you'd love to have?

Only Action Cures Fear

*Y*ou don't clear the fear to do the things. You do the things to clear the fear.

Remember when you were a kid on the diving board above a pool, overthinking it? That's what we do when it comes to so many things that scare us. Go back to that childhood moment or a similar one. How did you get over the paralyzing fear of jumping?

It wasn't by reviewing a pros-and-cons list. Or by mustering the strength over a twenty-four-hour period and trying again the next day. Or by thinking diving boards are stupid and playing in your room instead. *If you try to avoid failure, you also avoid success.*

There's no way around this one! When we understand that confidence is a willingness to be uncomfortable, we take more action. And the fear disappears. Because it has to. It cannot withstand your (albeit momentarily uncomfortable) action. And where does the fear go? Toward your next challenge! Action by action, you create an expansive life.

The fear never goes away, and the diving boards never get smaller. So somersault anyway.

137

You're Apologizing Too Much

*H*ave you ever noticed the overuse of the word *sorry*, especially by women? We overapologize like crazy! Here are some easy replacements:

- Instead of saying, "So sorry I'm a couple of minutes late," you can say, "Thank you for waiting!"
- Instead of saying, "Sorry I messed up," you can say, "I'll fix that right now, thanks for pointing it out!"
- Instead of saying, "Sorry to bother you," you can say, "Hey, do you have a moment?"

Saying "sorry" is often a reflex, but it doesn't have to be. You're meant to take up space in this world! There's no prize for being small or unbothersome. Words have power. And so do you.

Qualifications Aren't Everything

*I*f you need advice on starting a business, who do you want giving it to you?

- The business-school professor who's never run a business
- The e-college dropout who's invested in or built a successful venture (or several)

This isn't to diss education on any level. Education is a beautiful and important thing. But experience counts for a lot, too. And how do we get experience? Through action. All of life is on-the-job training, when you think about it. But we're so quick to discount experience, aren't we? We can stop doing that right now.

The meek won't inherit the earth. The action takers will. There are people in the world less qualified than you, doing what you're dreaming of doing, because they decided to bet on themselves! It's "let it be easy, follow your desire" versus "let me think of all the reasons this is bad idea and won't work."

Think less!

There's an old quote I love, "God doesn't call the qualified, God qualifies the called." You're not here by accident or just to take up space. You're already qualified *because you're alive.*

139

Closure Requires Only One Person

*M*y friend Stephanie was in an on-again, off-again relationship for more than three years. Her boyfriend had kids, an ex wife, and a permanent, hot-cold "it's complicated" status. (I've said it before and I'll say it again: avoid gray areas!) We were having our nails done apple-red, sitting side by side in a Lower Manhattan nail salon, when she exclaimed, "I just need Sam to give me closure! We haven't talked in weeks since he said he's not ready for the next step. I need clarity with him to put this whole confusing mess to bed."

I smiled. Said nothing. We'd been here before. When your emotions are high, it's hard to engage the mind. But wisdom involves engaging the heart *and* the head.

Stephanie said, "Why aren't you saying anything? This sucks!"

I paused and thought for a moment, then said, "Steph. You don't need closure from him. You can have it right this second. It only needs you to say, *That's it. It's closed.*"

A wound stays open when you keep prodding and investigating it.

Without your attention and interest, it closes itself up and heals just fine.

140

You Don't Have to Finish
What You Start

I once went to see Arianna Huffington speak in New York City.
I'll never forget something she said that day: "Sometimes the
best way to complete a project is to drop it."

Oh, sweet relief, the best human emotion! She was telling a
story about how she had plans to learn to ski and learn German
and more ... and my guess is that over the years these plans started
to make her feel bad or like she was falling behind.

Do you have to do all the things you once had a stirring desire
to do? Heck, no! Life changes. *Priorities change.* What was com-
pelling once might not be relevant for you anymore.

Here are some projects I've completed by dropping them:

- Learning sign language (maybe in the future)
- Mastering makeup via online tutorials (eh, mine is good
  enough)
- Reading the classics (if I don't dig them twenty or so pages
  in, I'm done)

- Seeing art galleries and museums in my city (I've realized I find most of them boring after fifteen minutes)

Trust your intuition regarding what's right for you to do and create next. You can say goodbye to anything and everything that no longer excites you.

You just got a *lot* of time back!

141

What You Don't Like in Someone Else, You Probably Don't Like in Yourself

This can be a tricky pill to swallow.

Carl Jung said, "Everything that irritates us about others can lead us to an understanding of ourselves."

Most of the time, we hold others to a standard that we impose on ourselves. I had a friend once with whom I had an instant spark. We both love to have fun, laugh, write, go out to bars, and meet new people. And then I said to Heath one day, "I love Nikki, but I've started to think she talks too much. I mean, she hogs the conversation."

He laughed. "No one talks more than you!"

Hmmmm.

Another time, when I was feeling a bit run-down, I snapped at a coworker for not pulling their weight on a deal we were closing. At that stage, the weight I was pulling was 60 percent of my usual go-go-go, do-do-do.

Once, a boss who was a total workaholic told me I was a "part-timer" when I left the office at 5:30 p.m. She always stayed after

8 p.m. Even in that stinging moment, I knew it had everything to do with her — and nothing to do with me.

I love what author Debbie Ford says in her book *The Dark Side of the Light Chasers*:

> We see only that which we are. I like to think of it in terms of energy. Imagine having a hundred different electrical outlets on your chest. Each outlet represents a different quality. The qualities we acknowledge and embrace have cover plates over them. They are safe: no electricity runs through them. But the qualities that are not okay with us, which we have not yet owned, do have a charge. So when others come along who act out one of these qualities they plug right into us.

I love to ask myself, *Am I upset for the reason I think I am? What's the real negative charge here?* What we shrug off one day might be an epic battle the next. Everything that annoys or triggers us about other people can lead us to a deeper understanding of who we are and of what's unhealed. When you have a negative charge toward someone, this is an invitation to learn more about yourself. Be curious. What might it be telling you about you? It's a gift.

The good news? This works in reverse, too! What you love, admire, respect, celebrate, and revere in another, you possess, too!

It's your own light being reflected back at you.

142

Doing It Is Easier Than Not Doing It

"*I* can't start a business / get going on a passion project / learn a new skill; it will take so long!" Guess what? *The time will pass anyway.*

We're very adept at talking ourselves out of going for our dreams. Seriously, look at how much life you have left. Are you fifty? You might live for fifty more years. The glass is half full. There's so much delicious life left to drink! So is it so hard to go for it — whatever "it" excites you? Be honest, now.

What are you kidding yourself about what's easy? Not allowing your desires to manifest? Not taking action on something new that calls to you? Letting time pass by while you wait for the "perfect time" to make a move or a change? There is no ideal time. Just time, and what you do with it. The conditions will never feel convenient.

I'll tell you what I think is hard. Working a job that doesn't excite you. Watching other people live their lives on TV while you tune in and let your days pass by. Creating stress and drama in your life as your resistance. Having an unmet dream in your heart that makes birthdays unpleasant. (I once heard a man say on his birthday, "I don't like to celebrate these — it's another year that my dreams get boxed out.") Ouch.

That's hard.

I once heard that the definition of hell is when the person you are meets the person you could have been. What if the person "you could have been" had it easier all along — with no regrets adding dead weight to their spirit? What if, in avoiding new challenges and opening yourself up to more, you're living the harder, less fun, shadow version of your temporary life experience?

Your desires won't go anywhere — no matter how much you diminish them or explain how unreasonable they might be. We don't live in a reasonable world. We live in a world where desires were invented to be brought to life.

Ever wonder why you have gifts that are aligned with your desire? Perhaps you love to sing and have a good singing voice. Or you love to solve problems and also possess an entrepreneurial flair. It's because that's what we're supposed to do with our gifts — give them away.

143

Be a Light for Others

*W*hen you intentionally allow more ease in, you're a light for others. You lead the way for those who are making their lives too hard, and that's a generous act. You're showing them that life can be lived in a gentler way. People think, *Hmm, how is she doing it? Could I be more like that? Could it all be more ... fun, simple, relaxed?*

Words don't light the way for others the same way that your energy and actions do. Your life is your example of what's possible for others. Ease naturally creates more ease.

Give yourself a break when things are hard or when you secretly sense that you might be making something harder. You can always come home to ease when you're ready. I write "this is it" on the first page of every new journal I break open. Because it's too easy to forget, and I want this perspective every morning when I open it.

This is it. Your life. It's happening now.

Look around you. Everything you see now once never was.

And one day it will all be gone. Your children, too, if you have them, and their children. You're hanging out on a blue marble that's spinning in the middle of an infinite universe. You're here for a short time, and like all things, you will be gone soon. It's a terrible shame to come to this realization at the end of your life instead of today.

Enjoying and allowing a full-life experience instead of struggling against it is the only logical thing to do, then, isn't it?

The world will tell you to hustle nonstop, produce, win, go-go-go, and earn anything worth having through sweat every step of the way. *But you don't have to buy into it.* Especially because now you know there is another way. You know ease is available at any moment. You can drop the illusion of emergency and drama. You can drop the belief that you need to sweat for every success, even though that's what people will tell you.

Your warmhearted readiness to be a force of ease in the world is powerful for everyone else, too. Because a person with the *let it be easy* wisdom elevates every room they enter. We seek them out consciously and subconsciously — because they embody this truth.

If you want to live your life in the most generous way, demonstrate more ease. See what happens. Pay attention to the strong, silent impact you make. Easier living is contagious. It's as if people are reminded of something ancient within them that they've known all along but haven't yet activated. You laugh more. You create and experience more joy. Stress evaporates. You might even live longer.

Now we're coming to the end of this book, and I'll admit — I'm resisting it. They say that you write the book you need to read. And in this moment, it feels true. It reminds me of a special exchange that happened right before Heath and I moved to New York from Sydney. We were having dinner with his family, and the mood was thick with emotion. His grandfather had passed not long before, and his grandmother Beryl sat quietly before us at the table — not saying much but looking at us with her loving, gentle eyes.

As we all hugged and laughed to relieve the heaviness of the moment, Grandma waited patiently near the door with a small, serene smile. I embraced her more closely than usual. I told her we'd come back as soon as we could to visit. I giggled when I asked her to please mail me her famous shortbread as soon as we had a new address.

Beryl nodded. Her serene smile did not move.

She touched my face with her soft, papery hands and said, "Have a wonderful life, darling."

Five words. The ultimate, simple wisdom from a great-grandmother who grew up during the Depression.

I had to hold back the tears until we buckled our seat belts.

I feel like I'm waiting at the door now, and you closing this book is your exit. And as I resist my goodbye to you, dear reader, can we both remember this together? When you think you've allowed ease in, *allow in even more.*

Have a wonderful life, darling.

And remember to pass it on.

About the Author

Susie Moore is a life coach and advice columnist for some of the world's biggest media outlets. A former sales director and adviser for start-ups in Silicon Valley and New York, she has had work featured in *Business Insider, Forbes, Entrepreneur, Marie Claire*, and the *Huffington Post*, and on *Today* and Oprah.com. She is the author of *Stop Checking Your Likes* and reaches her audience online and in person with workshops, newsletters, and media appearances, including podcasts. A native of England, she now lives and works in Miami.

NEW WORLD LIBRARY is dedicated to publishing books and other media that inspire and challenge us to improve the quality of our lives and the world.

We are a socially and environmentally aware company. We recognize that we have an ethical responsibility to our readers, our authors, our staff members, and our planet.

We serve our readers by creating the finest publications possible on personal growth, creativity, spirituality, wellness, and other areas of emerging importance. We serve our authors by working with them to produce and promote quality books that reach a wide audience. We serve New World Library employees with generous benefits, significant profit sharing, and constant encouragement to pursue their most expansive dreams.

Whenever possible, we print our books with soy-based ink on 100 percent postconsumer-waste recycled paper. We power our offices with solar energy and contribute to nonprofit organizations working to make the world a better place for us all.

Our products are available wherever books are sold. Visit our website to download our catalog, subscribe to our e-newsletter, read our blog, and link to authors' websites, videos, and podcasts.

customerservice@newworldlibrary.com
Phone: 415-884-2100 or 800-972-6657
Orders: Ext. 110 • Catalog requests: Ext. 110
Fax: 415-884-2199

www.newworldlibrary.com